ON THE
LEFT HAND
OF CHRIST

On The Left Hand of Christ,
How We Created Lori Vallow Daybell
© 2025 Tom Evans

Photo credits: Tom Evans, Susan Evans

ISBN (hardcover): 979- 8- 9925688- 6- 8
ISBN (paperback): 979- 8- 9925688- 7- 5
ISBN (ebook): 979- 8- 9925688- 8- 2
ISBN (audiobook): 979- 8- 9925688- 9- 9

Published by Tom Evans Contact the author at
tomevansauthor@gmail.com

ON THE LEFT HAND OF CHRIST

HOW WE CREATED LORI VALLOW DAYBELL

Book 3 in The Murder Trials of Chad Daybell
and Lori Vallow Daybell Series

TOM EVANS

Juror #18 in the Lori Vallow Daybell Trial

"...AFTER ALL, IT WAS YOU AND ME"
Quote from Rolling Stones song:
Sympathy For the Devil

32 And there were also two other, malefactors, led with him to be put to death.

33 And when they were come to the place, which is called Calvary, there they crucified him, and the malefactors, one on the right hand, and the other on the left.

(Luke 23: 32-33, KJV)

39 And one of the malefactors which were hanged railed on him, saying, if thou be Christ, save thyself and us.

40 But the other answering rebuked him, saying, Dost not thou fear God, seeing thou art in the same condemnation?

41 And we indeed justly; for we receive the due reward of our deeds: but this man hath done nothing amiss.

42 And he said unto Jesus, Lord remember me when thou comest into thy kingdom.

43 And Jesus said unto him, Verily I say to thee, Today shalt thou be with me in paradise.

(Luke 23: 39-43 KJV)

CONTENTS

PART II

The Trials of Lori Vallow Daybell

113

FORWARD

Jesus was crucified and died on the cross for our sins. Two other men were crucified on that most fateful day in the history of mankind. Dismas to Jesus' right and Gestas to his left. Both were thieves. On Jesus' right, Dismas was repentant. On Jesus' left, Gestas was not. Jesus reassured Dismas, telling him he would be in paradise with Jesus that day, but Gestas was unrepentant and mocked Jesus. He didn't ask for forgiveness before he died on his cross, and so, he went to Hell.

Lori Vallow Daybell is most obviously guilty of committing horrific crimes. She conspired to commit the murders of Charles, Tammy, JJ and Tylee of her own free will. We have committed her to prison for the rest of her life. We all despise what she did. Like Gestas, she is unrepentant and mocks Jesus when she claims to have a personal relationship with him.

However, putting her in prison can't be the end of it. We have to look inward and understand how we as a civilized society, produce people like her and Chad Daybell. How do we continue to produce school shooters, church shooters, mall shooters, subway cut-throats, political assassins, murderous religious zealots, the destroyers of innocents?

We can't leave it up to police, prosecutors or politicians. The answers have to come from us, the free citizens of our unique and wonderful democratic republic. We are the ones who decide the direction our country takes. We are the voters, the influencers, the voice.

So, it's up to us to understand the cultural waves behind the crazy people. What shoves them in a direction so far from reality that they can do the unthinkable. Why do they think the way they do? What influences took hold of their minds and drove them?

I don't claim to have the answers, but I hope to inspire thought, an introspection into ourselves, hopefully a change in direction.

We have to be willing to ask ourselves hard questions. We have to be unafraid of controversy. We have to be less offended by opposing views. We need free public discourse. Our future depends on it. The very existence of our free country depends on it.

As I write this it's been over two years since I served as a juror in the Lori Vallow Daybell (LVD) trial in Idaho. In spite of the horrors my fellow jurors and I were exposed to, I cannot imagine sitting through a more interesting trail. We were given a glimpse into a dangerous world of religious zealotry and I realized that LVD was part of a bigger problem. By the time she was sentenced I had determined to do my part in exposing what I believe the problems are, and writing about it in an effort to explain it to the rest of the world.

I wrote about her crimes in *Money, Power and Sex*. I'm going to just briefly recount them here without reliving the brutality. Just know that LVD, her brother Alex Cox and Chad Daybell brutally murdered the very people they were supposed to love, cherish and protect.

On July 11, 2019 Alex shot and killed LVD's husband Charles Vallow in Chandler, AZ. In spite of the fact that Charles had previously called police, clearly telling them he thought LVD and her brother Alex wanted to murder him, and in spite of all the evidence pointing to murder, Alex and LVD were not arrested. LVD wasn't charged with conspiracy to murder of Charles in AZ until June, 2021, after she was charged for murder in Idaho.

On September 9, 2019 LVD's daughter Tylee Ryan was brutally murdered and buried in Chad's backyard in Rexburg, ID. On September 22, 2019 LVD's son, JJ Vallow was murdered and buried in Chad's backyard.

On October 19, 2019 Chad's wife Tammy Daybell was murdered at home in her bed. Her death was initially thought to be of natural causes. The medical examiner later exhumed her body and changed the cause of death to homicide.

Chad, LVD and Alex were not done. On October 2, 2019 Alex narrowly missed shooting Brandon Boudreaux in the head in Gilbert, AZ. Brandon was uninjured and lived to testify against his then wife's aunt and her husband.

If you want to know how these murders were committed, I went through the timeline, brutality and details of these murders in my previous two books.

Our understanding of LVD's murders of innocents is just the beginning of understanding a much bigger problem. Innocent children are being murdered, enslaved, trafficked and abused continually in our free republic. We should be doing more to put a stop to it.

Whatever your feelings are about religious freedom, polygamy, Mormon fundamentalism and personal choice, our laws are being broken and people are being hurt in the name of it all. Crimes against innocents are still crimes even when they are done by people claiming to have a higher religious standing than the rest of us. It's time we put an end to it.

INTRODUCTION

Welcome to my third book about the almost unexplainable murders of Charles Vallow, Tylee Ryan, JJ Vallow and Tammy Daybell. Thank you for being patient with me and sticking with me while I attempt to explain what led Lori Vallow Daybell, Chad Daybell and Alex Cox to commit these horrible, uncalled for murders. And thank you for your interest in who else might be complicit in these murders. Who might have known something, who could have saved lives or at the very least, who could have helped solve the mystery of the missing children as desperate anguished loved ones searched for them before they were found buried in Chad Daybell's backyard.

I promise not to hash over the same ideas I share in the first two books. Hopefully you read those books before you read this one. You need that background to understand what I write here.

In my first two books I wrote about my experience as a juror. In book two I mentioned that I was just beginning to come to terms with it all personally. I find that I am still in that process. I'm still learning more about myself and my reaction to what I initially was exposed to and what I now immerse myself in. In spite of the fact that I served with 17 other jurors, serving on a jury like the one I served on is in most ways a personal journey.

Why do I do it? I said in book one it was because I wanted to share the good I found in law enforcement and the court system in Idaho, and I wanted to tell about my experience. In book two I said it was because I wanted to share new insights and how my thoughts had evolved.

All three books, though, are written in my attempt to explain not why, but *how* a mother could murder her children in the most brutal way and feel perfectly okay with it.

Trying to answer that question has challenged me in ways I couldn't have expected. I knew when I first asked the question to myself that it was a complex question, and I knew there were no easy answers.

The answer might seem to be that well, she's crazy. But, she's not. At least not in a way that keeps her from being able to reason. And, that would be too easy. That would let us all off the hook. We could just write her off, put her away for the rest of her life and move on. I'm really hoping that's not what's happening here. If we do that, if we put her in prison and pat ourselves on the back for a job well done, justice served, and just forget about her, we are not getting to the root of the problem and it *will* happen again. Or maybe a better way to say it is that it will continue to happen. We are fooling ourselves if we don't admit that crimes against innocent children, horrible, brutal crimes committed ostensibly in the name of religion, are happening in our country continually.

Tylee and JJ just happened to have a Kay Woodcock who wouldn't let things go when she suspected they may be in danger. And LVD (Lori Vallow Daybell) just happened to choose to come to Idaho to commit three of her crimes. Big mistake.

Unfortunately, not all family units are what we would hope they would be. Not all children have parents, grandparents, brothers, sisters, aunts and uncles to watch out for them and protect them if they are in danger.

Not all states have systems in place that are capable of protecting those children. Unfortunately, and in spite of the good people in all states who work within those systems, the systems themselves fall short of what they are meant to be, what they are expected to be. It's the leadership at the very top levels where the problems lie. Or, maybe a better way of saying that is that the problem lies with us. How we vote, what our priorities are, our lack of understanding what is really going on.

I listened to a discussion not long ago that turned into an argument. Person one claimed that people today are so much smarter and more knowledgeable than our founding fathers were. He went on to say that the average American spends more time in school, we have easier access to more news and we are just all around more worldly.

Person two said that's a farce. In the beginning I was siding with person one. I thought it was obvious. So much so, that I had never given it any thought. It seemed to make sense that of course we were better educated in the 21st century than someone in 1776. Our world view is surely wider than someone living in the 1700s. After all, we have the internet and cable news. In the 1700s they didn't even have the telegraph yet. It took months to find out what was happening in other parts of the world and sometimes weeks to find out what was happening in other parts of our country.

As person two explained his position though, I began to understand his point. We do have access to all kinds of outlets, but we are exposed to so much misinformation that our view of reality is skewed. Even in school we hear what the institution and the teacher or professor want us to hear. If we get our news primarily from say CNN, we get their skewed version of events. If we watch Fox we get the other side. Unfortunately, a lot of younger people get their news from Facebook, TikTok and X or other outlets on their device. Who ever really knows what the truth is?

So, according to person two, we are not better educated. We are more misinformed. The world was simpler in the time of the birth of our country and the founding fathers understood it better than we understand our world today. The founding fathers generally had a more well-rounded education. They were better informed about what was going on in the world. I would add to all of that that we are hit with so much information, true and untrue, that it's hard for the American electorate to know what to think.

The reason behind person one's position was that we should not put too much importance in our constitution. We are more knowledgeable now and we should feel free to change it. It should be a living document. I'm going to use this platform to share with you my opinion: Our constitution is what gives us the rights and freedoms we have. It is unique in that. We as Americans are unique because of it. I could go on, but I'll spare you.

It's also rare to have a candidate for office, president, senator, state senator, judge, whatever, who clearly states what the real problems are and their solution to it. It's always more government or less government, raise taxes or cut taxes, war or no war. For sure no one runs on a platform of cleaning up the problems associated with religion.

We could say LVD is evil. I can tell you that if evil exists it certainly does reside in Lori Vallow Daybell. In all my life I had never been exposed to what I would call pure evil until I was confronted with her. I have been shot at point blank by a complete stranger. I have seen horrible things happen to innocent people. I guess I have life experience that comes with living a full, long life, but none of those things felt evil to me. Not dark, heavy and satanic. LVD does. But what drives that? Is she possessed by the devil?

Again, I don't think it's that simple and that would keep us from discovering what really drove her. Certainly, she is evil and maybe she is possessed by the devil or whatever evil force exists in our world, but if that's true, what led her to that? What doors opened in her mind to let that evil force take over? Whether it's the devil or if she's crazy, we still need to understand what drove her to that place.

In my first book I made the claim that Lori Vallow Daybell's motives were money, power and sex. She used her religion in order to gain those things and excuse her crimes.

Even if her motives were money, power and sex, her religion was actually the driving force behind her crimes. Mormonism is a powerful force in our country. Its original doctrine has unfortunately been the basis for a lot of the off-shoots of the Church of Jesus Christ of Latter-day Saints, and a lot of the groups that have cropped up; prepper groups, Facebook groups, near death experience groups, energy healing groups and more.

Chad Daybell and LVD clearly used the Mormon religion to not just excuse their crimes, but as the motivation behind their murders of their spouses and LVD's children. The Mormon Church has remained eerily silent about Chad and LVD. When Chad and LVD committed their murders, they were members in good standing of the Mormon Church. More importantly, their victims were members of the Mormon Church.

The Mormon Church's silence is inexcusable to me and gives us some insight into how we created a Chad and LVD. In Idaho, Tylee, JJ and Tammy were cherished members of the Mormon Church. The church didn't protect them while they were alive and they certainly are doing nothing to protect their memory.

And what of other children in danger? Two kids are missing right now after having been kidnapped. We know they have been taken by the FLDS (Fundamentalist Church of Jesus Christ of Latter-day Saints). We know they are in danger. We know children are being raped, enslaved and trafficked. Why does the Mormon Church remain silent? The only answer is the answer I have given before. It's a systematic (at the very least) belief that it is in the best interest of the church to keep out of it.

But the Mormon Church's biggest crime is that they are doing nothing, and I mean nothing to keep it from happening again. Every father who loves their children should be questioning the Mormon Church. If you're Mormon and you're offended by an outsider's criticism of your church, maybe your priorities are skewed by your own belief in a church that has obviously lost track of why it even exists in the first place.

The dangerous book *Visions of Glory* is still being used by professors at Brigham Young University. The idea that a man can have revelations from God is still a belief held by the church. I could go on with what I think are the problems historically, but the real existing problem with the Mormon Church right now is that it values its own existence above the children it serves. By doing so, it is putting its own children in danger just like the FLDS does.

FLDS fathers give up their daughters to old men like Warren Jeffs and Sam Bateman because it improves their standing in the church. Does the same problem exist in the mainstream LDS Church? I know it's a terribly offensive idea. But, if we're saying that what is best for the Mormon Church is to sweep Chad and LVD's crimes under the rug, we are putting children at risk and we are putting the Church above the safety and well-being of our children.

Maybe it's time that we rethink how we feel about the Mormon Church and Christianity in general. I believe in Christianity. I consider myself a Christian. But, just for the sake of thought let's look at it. Our country is founded on Christianity and I think we would not last long without it. I love the story of Christ and I think humanity is lost without it.

But what if we lived our lives differently? What if we quit thinking about an afterlife and focused more on the here and now. I'm not saying we should quit being Christians. I'm saying maybe we shouldn't live our lives for what comes after.

LVD was able to ignore her children and eventually murder them because she was thinking that life here on earth is just our mortal probation. The afterlife is so much more important. Our life here on earth is solely to prepare us for heaven. She was willing to do anything and believe anything that would in her eyes, get her closer to that goal. She lost all desire to do anything for her kids in this life.

What if we spent more time just being good human beings and less time praying and hoping God will step in and make things better? In a way it would be a more Christian way to live. Be helpful, be a good example, be a good role model, follow the ten commandments, strive to make your life and the lives of those around you better. Work hard and improve yourself, but don't ever do it at someone else's expense. Lift up those around you. Especially those who oppose you or are in competition with you. Your life will be better for it. It's what Jesus taught us to do.

Jesus didn't say to spend 3 hours in church on Sundays. He didn't tell us to tithe 10% of our income. He told us to wash the feet of those who serve us. He told us to be good to our neighbors, don't steal, don't cheat, praise God in our own way.

So, my purpose for writing this book is to expose what the problems are. They go deep. They are embedded in our history and in our culture. Our story begins in 1823 in New York State. We have to understand those times and the people who lived in them. We have to work our way through over 200 years of religion, history and culture and finally find ourselves in present times with at least the beginning of an understanding of how we created a monster and how that monster used her religion to manipulate people into committing the most horrific crimes on her behalf.

We think about the story of Jesus and how he was murdered. Who murdered Jesus? We think of Pontius Pilate and Judas. But the moral of that story is that *we* did. You and I. The same goes for Abraham Lincoln and JFK. We created a culture in which someone felt justified in murdering a president of the United States.

Our immediate response to those murders is to run down the culprit and make him pay for his crimes. Looking at it from an historical perspective with all the information that has been gathered over time, gives us the opportunity to study in depth, what led an assassin like John Wilkes Booth or Lee Harvey Oswald to commit their crimes.

The same goes for our story about Lori Vallow Daybell and Chad Guy Daybell. We could have said that Booth or Oswald were just crazy zealots and left it at that. But we didn't. We have been studying those crimes continually since they were committed. At least hundreds and probably thousands of books have been written. And, studying them has given us not only a somewhat better understanding of why they occurred, but also has helped keep them from occurring again.

Are Tylee and JJ's lives any less important than Lincoln or Kennedys? Are our children less valuable than our presidents? I think we agree the answer, of course, is no. So we keep studying and striving to understand if not LVD and Chad, at least what drove them. We do so in an effort to keep other children safe. It's all we can do and it's our burden to bear. We find ourselves in a place and a time and we won't find ourselves wanting.

So here we go:

PART I

WE CREATED A MONSTER

1

IN THE BEGINNING

To understand Mormonism and how it first came to be, we have to first understand the mood and the culture in our country in the 1820s and 1830s in what we have come to refer to as "the turbulent era". Poverty and instability were the norm at that time and people needed something they could latch onto. It's kind of the opposite of how we live now in the 21st century where the poorest of the poor in the US are better off than most people who lived in the early 1800s.

The vast majority of people had no education. Their options in life were limited to the labor they could perform with their physical strength. If a man were lucky enough, he could learn a trade that would raise him above the level of laboring 12 to 16 hours a day, 6 or 7 days a week. But just barely. Farming primarily and factory work becoming more prevalent, were his options.

If a woman was lucky, she would find a man who could support her and the many children that would inevitably come wanted or not. Even if she did, the financial support supplied by her husband would be just barely enough to feed and house the family.

Medical care was poor at best and very often non-existent. If you had a cavity, it would eventually result in a rotten tooth and the best you could hope for is to find someone who was willing to pull it for you. Usually that would be the local barber. He would give you a shot of whiskey (if you were lucky), have someone hold you down, and pull the offending tooth with a pair of pliers. If you were sick, you might easily die and a lot of people did die of things we just find annoying today. And, death didn't happen in a hospital or any kind of medical facility attended by physicians with pain reducing drugs.

In those days the US Government wasn't expected to or even capable of providing any kind of safety net for anyone. Things were no better in Europe. Colonialism was what had driven the economy of most of the European countries and it wasn't working as well as it once had.

Where would someone turn if they were in need of help? Many people found themselves in desperate situations, unable to feed themselves and their families. On top of that lawlessness was rampant. If you lived in one of the cities and found yourself on the street, you were at the mercy of the pickpockets, thieves and dirty cops looking to improve their own desperate situation at your expense. If you lived out west, which was pretty much anything west of the original thirteen colonies besides Chicago and St. Louis, you were at the mercy of marauding bands of "Indians", and all kinds of desperados and outlaws.

So, if in your ignorance and desperation someone approached you claiming to have answers to your problems, your best option might be to tie your hitch to his wagon and go wherever he leads you.

This situation in turn gave rise to many people who claimed to have answers to your problems and in reality, some of them did, in spite of their selfish purposes. Snake oil salesmen could cure your ills or at least ease your pain with alcohol or opium. Farmers in need of cheap labor could feed you and your family and religious hucksters could provide you with a community of people who could work together to better your circumstances.

In 1823 Joseph Smith was directed by the Angel Moroni to a hill near his home in New York State where he found the golden plates buried in a stone box. He later translated those plates with the help of a "seer" stone, from the Egyptian language into the Book of Mormon, and began gathering his flock. He claimed to be the one true prophet with direct communication to God. The Second Coming of Christ was at hand and it would be the Saints who would be prepared.

Russel M. Nelson, President of the Mormon Church until he died on September 27, 2025 quoted the prophets as saying:

"Possibly the most singular event to occur on the earth since the Resurrection," and it was "the greatest event in world history since the birth, ministry, and resurrection of Jesus Christ."

Nelson was talking about Joseph Smith's visitation by God and Jesus. In the two years leading up to Moroni guiding him to the golden plates, Joseph Smith talked to God, Jesus and angels several times.

Nelson is speaking about Smith's "first vision." Smith was visited by God and Jesus and it was the first time since the resurrection that God and Christ had revealed themselves to mortal man. This first vision occurred in 1820 and is the basis or foundation of the Mormon faith. God spoke directly to Joseph Smith. Joseph Smith is a prophet. There can be prophets on earth who get revelations and speak directly to God.

His story resonated with a lot of people of the time. It's hard to say whether they actually believed his stories in the beginning or if the roots of the Mormon Church were more out of necessity. Whatever the origin, Mormonism took hold and quickly began to grow.

Some at the time just thought Smith was a huckster. They tried to discredit him by exposing his past. He had claimed to be able to find gold. He called himself a "money digger" or treasure hunter. He claimed to be able to use a "seer stone" to find buried treasure or gold.

Whatever criticism anyone had, Joseph Smith was smart. As soon as he gathered a following and created the Mormon Church, he quickly set up a system of missionaries, eventually sending them all over the world to gather his flock. Polygamy might also have been a tool Smith used to grow his church.

Smith and Mormonism weren't the only men or religions gathering people in that time. It's complicated to explain the mood of the time. A lack of education and financial desperation gave rise to an overall feeling that there must be something more to life. There must be a point to all of the suffering. This led to people being open to ideas that the vast majority of us find hollow and ridiculous today.

Revivals were common. Preachers were everywhere gathering souls to their own brand of religion. Because of the hardships listed above and the inability for people to make it on their own, there were many religious groups popping up. It was similar to the communes of the 1960s. People could pool their resources and actually be successful farming land. They could share what little they had and make it work. There was safety in numbers, so they were less susceptible to crime.

Most of the men and sometimes men along with their wives, gathering souls, were not as successful as Smith. Whether that was because the story he was telling was the truth, or because he had his story more well thought out, is an ongoing debate. The Mormon Church today seems to fall on faith. Don't question Joseph Smith's story. It doesn't matter if it sounds unbelievable. It's a matter of faith.

Either way, Smith succeeded in gathering a flock and the Church of Jesus Christ of Latter-day Saints was founded in 1830. It was very successful and grew rapidly until people in surrounding communities began to feel overwhelmed by the sheer numbers of Mormons. The problem was that the Mormons could act as a group, vote as a group and basically take over communities. Joseph Smith had complete control and authority over his flock. His word, as he said, was the word of God. Disobeying Smith meant disobeying God and that was not tolerated. All Smith had to do was tell his followers who or what to vote for and they did it.

As you would expect, this kind of power over local politics and community issues began to have a negative effect on people outside of the Mormon Church. The more tension this caused, the more the Mormons became isolated. Because of this, it was easy for people to either outrightly make up stories about the Mormons or to believe things about the Mormons that weren't necessarily true.

One of the many rumors that were spread was of polygamy. Mormons didn't publicly introduce polygamy until the 1840s, but it is suspected that Joseph Smith and possibly others were practicing polygamy before then. It was considered a barbaric practice at the time. People held strong puritanic beliefs about marriage and religion and could not tolerate polygamy or any form of marriage other than a man and a woman. At least not out in the open.

It's well known that many slaveholding plantation owners in the south had in reality more than one wife. Their "legitimate", legal and white wife who everyone knew to be the mother of the plantation owner's children, but also oftentimes a black wife. This "wife" wouldn't be legal, wouldn't be given a choice, and her children would be considered bastards, unworthy of any of their father's wealth or even his name.

All of the tension and persecution forced the Mormons from New York and in 1831 they moved to Ohio and then to Missouri. They were eventually forced from those states also and ended up in Nauvoo, Illinois. Joseph and his brother Hyrum were murdered there in a political uprising after destroying the office of a newspaper that opposed them, and Brigham Young was elected to take over as the Prophet of the Church of Jesus Christ of Latter-day Saints.

It seems as though the Mormons were pushed west along with the expansion of the country. Civilized people just couldn't tolerate the Mormons, their strange ideas and their influence over politics. Brigham Young decided it was time to move further west into an area of the country where they would be left alone. It wasn't an easy choice and would be a hardship on his followers who had already suffered so much.

Leaving any of the communities they left was not by their choice. Their homes and crops had been burned, their deeds had been confiscated and they lost everything they had worked so hard for. By the time they started immigrating west to the Salt Lake Valley, hardship was nothing new to them and they found their strength only in their numbers.

Between 1856 and 1860 more than 3,000 Mormon Handcart Pioneers made the journey to the Salt Lake Valley. Many died on the way of exposure and exhaustion. They were too poor to even afford mules or oxen to pull a wagon, so they pulled the wagons filled with their children, elderly and whatever belongings they had, themselves. It was a heroic effort, and the Mormons celebrate them annually to this day.

This is the briefest explanation of early Mormon history and what brought them to Salt Lake. There is so much written about it and I encourage you to read more. It's very interesting and brings a reader a lot of understanding about early American history and the westward expansion. It also gives a broader understanding of Mormonism today. It is enough however, for the purposes of this book. You know that what brought the Mormons to Salt Lake was persecution, murder, theft and an overall intolerance of their beliefs. What made it grow so fast was the security it provided along with a well thought out missionary system not only in the US, but also China, Europe, India, South America and even South Africa.

2

THE MORMONS SETTLE IN SALT LAKE

One of the most notorious events in early Mormon history is the massacre that took place about 300 miles south of Salt Lake in an isolated valley surrounded by mountains known as Mountain Meadows. Before we get to that we need to understand what led up to it and what the mindset of the Mormons was at the time.

It's an event that has been shrouded in mystery for over 150 years. One reason for that is that the Civil War broke out shortly after the Mountain Meadows massacre and the country was distracted. The other big reason, as you will see, is that the Mormons involved twisted the truth and told outright lies about it. It happened in a remote part of the country and communication only happened when people traveled through carrying news with them. There was no telegraph in that part of the country yet, so express riders were the fastest mode of communication. They were generally young men of slight build on a fast horse.

As we know the Mormons had been pushed off of their farms and from their homes. They had lost everything they had worked so hard for several times. Salt Lake was their last hope and they had decided that they would never allow themselves to be removed. They would fight to the death if it came to that.

Brigham Young said to his followers:

"God has shown me that this is the spot to locate this people, here is where they will prosper..."

Of course, they moved there hoping to live in peace, free to practice their religion and live their lives in the way they chose. Brigham Young wanted Salt Lake to be self -governed. He wanted his word to be the law of the land. This would be a community built by Mormons for Mormons. There would be nobody to offend or contend with except a few local natives. Certainly, no organized form of government that could be turned against them.

The Mormons were industrious and organized. They laid out the Salt Lake Valley into sections like a grid that is still in use to this day. They also had a well- planned militia. Brigham Young was at the head of it all and his word was law. He put men he trusted into positions of power and spread them out over what we now know as Utah. Communities were built in strategic areas. Not just to protect and control commerce and the flow of goods through and into the territory, but also to farm, mine and log the resources that would be needed to build and grow. Utah has vast forests, valuable mineral deposits and millions of acres of farm and ranch land.

One of the historically problematic ideas or pursuits of the Mormon Church in the early years has been a dichotomy between using the U.S. Government to its advantage while wanting to be free to practice their religion in conflict with its laws. It was to Young and the Mormon's advantage for Utah to be a U.S. Territory because of the privileges that came with being a territory, but Young wanted to be free to run Utah however he saw fit. This is what led to what unfolded next.

By 1857 word had gotten to the Mormons that President Buchanon was sending troops to Salt Lake. As the army led by Gen. William Harney marched toward Utah, Young sent spies to find out what their purpose was. When the spies returned, they reported overhearing the troops saying they would "scalp old Brigham". This of course put the Mormons on edge. It is true that President Buchanon was sending troops to end polygamy and replace Brigham Young as governor.

Mormon Apostle Heber C. Kimball gave a speech which he ended by saying:

"Bring 2,500 troops here. I have wives enough to whip out the United States for they will whip themselves."

Mormons living outside of the Salt Lake valley were called home to reinforce the ranks and Native Americans living in the area were called upon to fight with the Mormons. The local Paiutes were suspicious of all white people but would always be willing to fight with whichever side they thought would benefit them the most.

The Mormons also overheard the troops say they would winter in Salt Lake. Past experience told them that meant the troops would exploit and "steal" Mormon women.

Gen. Harney had a reputation as an Indian fighter. He was known to show no sympathy when attacking Native American villages killing women and children as quickly as men, leaving nothing in his path but death and destruction.

Young was to be removed as governor of Utah Territory. The spies had heard that Gen. Harney intended to be governor of Utah and would enforce martial law on the Mormons. On top of that Parley P. Pratt, one of the Quorum of Twelve Apostles of the Church of Jesus Christ of Latter-day Saints, had been murdered in Arkansas by the estranged husband of a woman who he had taken in as his twelfth wife. The Mormons thought of Pratt as a martyr, having saved the woman from an abusive alcoholic husband.

The Mormons who lived in the Salt Lake Valley pioneered the land, fought off and tamed the natives and built it up for themselves. They had no intention of sharing it with anyone who wasn't Mormon. They had come voluntarily to end the persecution they had suffered in the east. They fully intended to live their lives by the Book of Mormon and the Bible and no outsider was going to be allowed to interfere with that.

There was understandably a lot of tension among the Mormons in Salt Lake when a wagon train on its way to California, which just happened to originate in Arkansas, the state where Pratt had just been murdered, primarily led by John Baker and Alexander Fancher, took the more southern route through Salt Lake. They were hoping to be resupplied by the Mormons there.

The route through Salt Lake wasn't the most used route, but it wasn't uncommon for emigrants to use it. The Mormons were known to have better supplies and feed than could be found at Fort Boise on the more northern route, even though they charged more for them. Trains could head southwest from Fort Laramie in Wyoming, go over South Pass in the Rocky Mountains down to Fort Bridger and on to Salt Lake. The trip from Fort Bridger to Salt Lake was only about 130 miles, but they were hard miles through the mountains. Ahead of them was the Great Salt Lake and the Great Basin and they would need to be in good condition, well stocked and rested to survive the trip.

By the time the train arrived in Salt Lake, Young had issued an order not to sell supplies to the wagon train. Not a kernel of grain nor an ounce of lead was to be sold or traded. I've always questioned why he would do that. He claimed to have no knowledge of the attack on the train and not to have ordered it. If he meant the party no harm, why wouldn't he allow them to resupply?

One answer might be that Young intended to stock up in preparation for General Harney's siege which he was sure was coming. Also, Utah had suffered two straight years of extreme drought. Farmers and livestock had yet to recover from that. But, the train was relatively rich and could afford the high prices the Mormons commonly charged people immigrating through on their way to California.

Being unable to resupply put the train in a dire situation. They had no choice in the matter though as few in the valley would disobey Young's order. The only thing they could do was ration what few supplies they had left and move on. They weren't even allowed to graze their stock in the Salt Lake valley. Mormons in Salt Lake and south of Salt Lake had claimed all the grazing land as their own whether they had a legal right to it or not. The Baker-Fancher party had a lot of working stock, but also a large herd of cattle they hoped to profit from in California. This caused a lot of tension between the Mormon settlers and the emigrants migrating through the area and led to some minor skirmishes. The next likely spot where they could graze their worn-out stock and refit and repair their wagons was Mountain Meadows 300 hard miles to the south.

What happened at Mountain Meadows has been studied thoroughly, yet still is shrouded in controversy. What is known, however, is that it was a completely uncalled for and brutal murder of 120 innocent men, women and children. On top of that, the children who were, considered to be, too young to tell about what happened were spared and farmed off to Mormon families. Some claim that the families took the children in to be charitable and raise them like their own. I think they saw the children as an asset they could use to work the farms. Those children were eventually recovered and returned to their relatives back east and some *were* able to tell about what they witnessed.

Shortly after arriving at Mountain Meadows the train was attacked by a group of Mormons and some of the Paiute Indians living in the area. A few members of the train were killed and some were injured in the initial attack. The Mormons led by Major John D. Lee and others had originally tried to get the Paiutes to attack the train on their own. They had been conditioning the Paiutes to side with them against the whites who they said were in league against both the Mormons and the Paiutes. The Paiutes were untrusting of the Mormons though, and reluctant to serve as their proxy in a battle they didn't necessarily support.

As it turned out the initial attack on the train was committed primarily by the Paiutes who were expecting to profit by stealing the train's supplies and livestock. Later, when the attack on the train proved to be more of a challenge than expected, the Mormons dressed up as Indians and attacked the train with only a little help from the Paiutes.

The relationship between the Paiutes and the Mormons, the Paiutes and the emigrants and the Paiutes and the U.S. Government was a fluid thing. The Mormons had developed a mostly peaceful arrangement with them. They traded with them and fought with them when it was mutually beneficial.

The Paiutes in the area left the emigrants alone usually, trading with them when they felt like it and stealing from them when there was an easy target. In turn, the emigrants were generally nervous to see any kind of Native American and some were just as likely to shoot without asking questions as not.

The U.S. Government didn't have a lot of influence over the natives in the area yet, but the natives knew enough to be untrusting. They knew there would be strings attached to whatever "gifts" were offered.

So, the question for the Paiutes was: fight with the U.S. Government against the Mormons, or with the Mormons against the U.S. Government. The Mormons were at least known to them. The Mormons also filled their heads with a lot of propaganda about the U.S. Government and the wagon train heading into their area.

The train was attacked and put under siege for several days. After the initial attack, the wounded suffered terribly from their wounds and from thirst. There was a creek just a short distance from the circled wagons. Some members of the party heroically made it to the creek while under intense fire and were able to bring some water back to the people huddled within the circled wagons, but it wasn't enough.

A few men had been able to escape from within the circled wagons and leave the area on horseback to get help. What happened to them when they came across the people they thought would help is very telling about the Mormons' part in the massacre.

Stake President and Iron County Militia Commander Isaac Haight had sent a detachment ostensibly to see for themselves and report back to him what was unfolding at Mountain Meadows. As it turned out, their real purpose was to support the Paiutes and keep encouraging them in their attack. The Mormons could not allow the two men who escaped the besieged wagon train to get word out about what was unfolding. As the men approached, they were shot in cold blood. The two men from the train had thought the Mormons would be their saviors. They couldn't have been more wrong.

Modern day photo of the creek adjacent to the site of the siege. Personal photo.

The problem faced by the Mormons now was that people within the train were aware of Lee and others participation in the attack. At this point it seems that the Mormons were looking for a way to end the siege. However, if the emigrants were allowed to leave the area they would tell the outside world about the Mormons' part in the attack. And the Mormons felt like the outside world was just looking for a reason to attack them.

Isaac Haight asked Col. William H. Dame what should be done. Col. Dame was in charge of the military in Parawan (a settlement near Mountain Meadows), mayor of Parawan and stake president of the LDS Church in Parawan, so we can assume his word carried a lot of weight. We don't know for sure if he gave Haight outright permission to murder the emigrants, but we do know that is what happened after Haight met with Dame. We also know that other trains bound for California were thought to be on their way into the area and would stumble upon the besieged train in Mountain Meadows. That would compound the problems for the Mormons and increase the danger of retaliation from the outside world.

Further, we know Buchannon's troops were on their way into Utah and thought by the Mormons to already be in southern Utah. We know now that the troops were nowhere near Utah. They were strung out in Kansas and Wyoming and wouldn't get to Utah that year. The Mormons, and especially the Mormons who perpetrated the attack, were in an impossible situation with no good options and were about to be found out.

We do know from journals and accounts that the idea of murdering everyone in the Baker-Fancher party was discussed among the Mormons. The problem is that there was so much confusion following the murders with everyone trying to cover up their part and excuse themselves. Passing the buck so to speak. Haight claimed that Dame gave the order to murder everyone and Dame claimed that Haight gave the order on his own.

There has always been a question as to what role Brigham Young played or if he even knew what his subordinates were up to. Remember Salt Lake City is 300 miles north of Mountain Meadows and the only mode of communication was by express rider. Most of what we know comes from the testimony of James H. Haslam taken 27 years later in1884.

Express rider Haslam was tasked with riding all the way from Cedar City to Salt Lake City and back. It was a grueling ride. Upon arriving in Salt Lake City and meeting with Brigham Young, he was given an hour to sleep while Young wrote his response to Haight. When Haslam returned an hour later Young told him:

"Brother Haslam, I want you to ride for dear life; ride day and night. Spare no horse flesh."

In Young's response he told Haight:

"You must not meddle with them."

That seems pretty clear. In his note to Haight, he clearly says to leave the emigrants alone. But, what of the Paiutes attacking the train? Young wanted the Paiutes and the emigrants to work out their differences without Mormon interference wherever that led. He also thought the emigrants, being well armed with very capable men, would be more than able to defend themselves against the Paiutes.

Those who claim that Young had a part in the massacre or at least was aware of what his subordinates were up to, say Young was just covering for himself. Young knew what was happening and that his dispatch would be too late to stop it.

It's obvious that most of the Mormons in positions of power in the area knew that Lee had attacked the train using the Paiutes and that he now intended to murder everyone in the train including women and children. Orders were given by militia leaders to their soldiers to go to Mountain Meadows and "bury the remaining emigrants". It was known to all what that meant since it was known that most of the emigrants were still alive and under siege. Also, some disobeyed orders and refused to go on the mission, giving further evidence that those who did go, knew what they were getting themselves into.

This is one of the most, if not the most clear example of the dangers of believing that some men have the voice of God in their heads. Some Mormons were reluctant to murder the emigrants in cold blood, but claimed or at least claimed to believe that their leaders had "the spirit of God and knew better what was right than they did." They either believed that God wanted them to murder the emigrants in cold blood to save themselves or they at least thought that idea excused them. (This is exactly how Chad and LVD convinced LVD's brother Alex to murder for them and how Warren Jeffs convinces fathers to give over their underage daughters 163 years later.)

After days of suffering for the emigrants, and in absolute desperation within the confines of the circled wagons, Mormons approached the train under a white flag of truce. To understand why the emigrants finally gave in, we have to understand what life was like for them in the summer sun in the impossibly small area they were doing their best to survive in. They had the dead bodies of their companions to deal with. The smell and the flies the dead bodies were attracting was overwhelming. They had several badly wounded whose agonizing screams and crying they had to contend with. They had nowhere to relieve themselves except within their small area. They were out of food and water and to top it all off they were about out of ammunition. Their situation was beyond hopeless.

The Mormons told the emigrants that the Paiutes agreed that if they surrendered their weapons, the Paiutes would allow the Mormons to escort them out of the area. The emigrants were not trusting of the Mormons and initially turned down the offer. In the end though, they felt they had no choice. They would surrender their weapons and everything they owned in exchange for their lives.

What happened next is the most brutal, uncalled for attack on innocent civilian Americans by Americans in our history. Because of the threat of Civil War and the eventual Civil War itself, back east, and because it was so unbelievable, it took years for the truth of what happened to finally sink in for people living outside of Utah.

Majors John D. Lee and John H. Higbee gave orders to the gathered Mormon militiamen. All of the emigrants except children too young to relay what happened later, were to be killed. They would be escorted from their camp under a flag of truce. A signal would be given by Higbee to halt at which time the militiamen were to kill the emigrant men. The Paiutes would dispatch the women and older children. The treachery committed by the Mormons on people who thought, or at least hoped, they were there to save them from the Paiutes is almost too much to comprehend.

The women and children were loaded into wagons and led over a rise about a mile to the south of the emigrant encampment. As soon as they went over the rise and were out of sight of the men, the men were marched single file with an armed Mormon by his side in the same direction. A signal was given and every one of the emigrant men was immediately executed in cold blood. As soon as that was done all of the women and children old enough to repeat what they had witnessed were summarily executed.

Rise to the south the women and children were taken over.
Personal photo.

All of the wealth owned by the emigrants; their cattle, equipment and children were divided up amongst the Mormons. A little was shared with the Paiutes to insure their complicity in the atrocity and keep them quiet. The bodies of 120 men, women and children were left to rot in the summer sun or buried in shallow graves, soon to be dug up by wolves and coyotes.

There are rumors of depredations committed on the women by John D. Lee and others, but unfortunately no real proof survived since no one was left to confirm the stories.

It was a full year before anyone from the U.S. Government came to Mountain Meadows to find out what happened there. What they found when they got there horrified them and convinced them that the rumors they had heard were true. Bones and skulls were strewn across the area. Pieces of clothing were stuck in the sagebrush. The cavalrymen did what they could to identify the victims, bury what remains they could gather and build a monument to the dead.

Old monument. Personal photo.

The Mormons initially denied their part in the Mountain Meadows massacre, but as time went on and the Civil War ended, people started looking for answers. The families of the victims wouldn't let the matter die.

When news of the slaughter reached people back east, they were horrified and angered against the Mormons. Justice, however, was slow in coming and extremely limited in its scope.

John D. Lee, Brigham Young's adopted son, would take the blame. Young had hoped to shield Lee by sending him south to run the ferry across the Colorado River on the express road between Utah and California. Lee spent several years there before being brought back to Mountain Meadows to be executed by a firing squad for his part in the Mountain Meadows massacre. As it turned out, Lee was the "fall guy" and paid the price for the many who were involved in the massacre.

Lee had loved Brigham Young and loved Utah. Before he died, he wrote a lot about the landscape he was immersed in around Lee's Crossing. It is a strikingly beautiful place with towering red cliffs overlooking the Colorado River.

On the morning of his execution Lee rose from his perch where he had been sitting on his coffin, to give a speech. I believe that one of the reasons the government went to the trouble of taking Lee all the way back to the remote Mountain Meadows is that they hoped he would open up and give information as to who else was complicit in the murders. He did not do that, but in his speech, I see the first *split* in the Mormon Church. Of Young, Lee says:

"I believe he is leading the people astray, downward to destruction, but I believe in the gospel that was taught in its purity and introduced by Joseph Smith in former days."

Lee's Crossing today. Personal photo.

Remains of the old fort dating from the time Lee lived there.
Personal photo.

Historic marker. Personal photo.

It hasn't changed since Lee's time. Personal photo.

Who knows for sure what Lee was alluding to, but it sounds to me like he is saying Brigham Young is straying under pressure from the original doctrine laid out by Joseph Smith, which would include polygamy. Lee himself had many wives and over 50 children. Indeed, Young did renounce polygamy later causing a split in the church which eventually led to the Church of the Firstborn and the FLDS (Fundamentalist Church of Jesus Christ of Latter-day Saints).

I have visited the Mountain Meadows Memorial twice and I will tell you it is a solemn place. I have been to the Custer Battlefield several times and studied the events that occurred there in depth. I have been to the sights of other massacres and battles that happened in the settling of the American west. None are as haunting as Mountain Meadows. The only location I have ever been that touched me as deeply as Mountain Meadows is Chad Daybell's backyard.

Overlooking Mountain Meadows. Personal photo.

Wagon tracks and possibly rifle pits. Personal photo.

Modern day memorial. Personal photo.

Grave sites are scattered around where remains were found. Personal photo.

A point to be made here is that LVD is very good at twisting the truth and telling outright lies in order to protect herself and justify her actions. The question arises: Is it a cultural thing? Mormons in 1857 were very good at shrouding the truth in lies and confusion to justify their actions and protect themselves. Many were able to excuse themselves for their crimes saying they were following the orders of people with a higher religious standing. Have those abilities been handed down through generations? That's the truth I'm trying to get at.

3

A SPLIT IN THE MORMON CHURCH

"There is a mouthpiece of God who will give you that certainty."
Dr. Christine Marie Katas quoting Warren Jeffs

Within any community there is a culture. Stories handed down through generations. A lot of the information we have about what occurred in Mountain Meadows in 1857 comes from ancestors of the perpetrators, some of whom still live in the area. Naturally, they claim that their particular ancestor was innocent or at least only following the orders of his superiors. I'm sure that's the excuse they were handed down, and in some cases, it is probably true. In other cases, I think they are lies told after the fact to cover for the atrocious acts of the ancestor. Whatever it is, it is only important to us in order to understand what drives Mormons today.

Joseph Smith claimed he was visited by divine beings and he was persecuted for it. The origin of that put them in an extremely defensive posture. It doesn't excuse them for Mountain Meadows, but it does help explain why they were so nervous about "outsiders", especially since their religion caused a divide between Mormons and gentiles and both sides had suffered from it. Mormons had been persecuted for their beliefs for a generation before 1857. They believed President Buchanon's troops were about to invade their territory.

Buchanon's troops never did attack the Mormons in Salt Lake. The country was tired of war and tired of fighting each other. The Civil War ended, President Lincoln was assassinated, John D. Lee was eventually executed and the country looked forward. The wounds caused by those events lingered in the minds of Americans though, and the effects sent us in different directions than may have been predicted.

Polygamy on its own may have been tolerated if not for Mountain Meadows. And if not for all of the injustices that accompanied it. "Stealing" other men's wives, the marrying off of underage girls and eventually receiving funds from the government meant to help single moms, all put pressure on Brigham Young and his followers. In the end, in order to keep his power, Brigham Young and the Mormons renounced polygamy even though many still practiced the principle in secret. In 1890, three years after Brigham Young's death, the LDS Church officially prohibited new plural marriages. In 1904 the LDS Church issued a manifesto officially renouncing polygamy and threatening to excommunicate any Mormons who practiced it.

But this caused a split in the Mormon Church. Many believed as John D. Lee apparently did, that the original doctrine written by Joseph Smith and told by him to be a revelation and the word of God, was their way into the Celestial Kingdom. Simply put, without at least three wives and as many children as a man and his wives could produce, a man would not make it to the Celestial Kingdom (Heaven in the Mormon world). In turn, his wives and children would not make it to Heaven. The priest-holder husband was their key.

There is obviously a more selfish reason to hold on to the doctrine of polygamy. An unlimited supply of younger wives to not only serve their husbands in the bedroom, but to supply children to work the farms, work themselves and multiply the flock. And for the church a never-ending supply of new members to grow the congregation.

Factions split off from the established church led by Brigham Young. There are many to this day. There are places still in this country primarily in Utah, Arizona, Montana and Idaho where polygamy is barely hidden and almost openly practiced. The Apostolic United Brethren (AUB) runs the tiny community of Pinesdale, Montana.

Pinesdale is an openly polygamist community in the beautiful Bitterroot Valley. I visited Pinesdale recently. It is much cleaner and more prosperous looking than Colorado City, but it has some of the same problems. The only school in Pinesdale is the one run by The Apostolic United Brethren. All of the property is owned by the AUB and there are ongoing disputes between the people who built their homes on the property and the AUB.

The AUB was founded in 1954 and is another offshoot of the Church of Jesus Christ of Latter-day Saints. They follow the original doctrine and practice polygamy.

The leader of the AUB, Lynn A. Thompson had been accused of sexual abuse by his daughter and two nieces. Thompson died in 2021. He was never convicted.

Pines Academy. Personal photo.

Bigamy; the practice of having more than one spouse, is a misdemeanor in Montana. In most states it's a felony, so in Montana, the price of plural marriage, if prosecuted, is less. Even though polygamy is illegal in Montana, law enforcement, prosecutors and politicians tend to look the other way, choosing to ignore the fact that the community openly breaks the law by practicing polygamy. I think it's a good indication, in Montana at least, that we are willing to let people live their lives the way they choose as long as they aren't abusing children or causing harm to anyone outside of their cult or church. The men and women living there, practicing polygamy are doing it of their own free will.

They settled and own the land they live on. They don't seem to go out of their way to influence the communities close to them and they aren't trying to expand their boundaries.

Do they "bleed the beast" by collecting government subsistence money meant for single moms? That might be the rub. It seems though that the AUB has its own welfare system and encourages its members to use it rather than rely on public assistance programs provided by the state of Montana. Maybe it's a little closer to the ideal than the FLDS.

Monteview, Idaho is an FLDS stronghold and is the town where the Fischer children were recently kidnapped by the FLDS. Boundary County in Idaho, on the Canadian border is known to be a highly polygamist community. And of course there is still Colorado City, Arizona and Hildale, Utah. It has become a political and law enforcement nightmare. Our constitution guarantees us the right to practice our religion in whatever way we choose. We can openly worship the devil if we choose. We can believe in and preach whatever we want. We can create communities based on our beliefs whether anyone likes it or not.

On the other hand, there are things that *are* illegal in our country. Polygamy is illegal. Forcing underage girls to marry is illegal. Human trafficking is illegal. Collecting welfare meant for single moms in order to live a life of polygamy is illegal. But on it goes. The attempts to come to terms with these crimes and put a stop to them has resulted in bad press for politicians causing the end of their political careers. Law enforcement and Child Protective Services have suffered funding cuts and ends of careers also.

The people running the offshoots of the Mormon Church have learned well how to use propaganda to their advantage causing a well-meaning, but misinformed public to turn against those who try to solve the problems.

It's nothing new in our country. Al Capone, Bonnie and Clyde Barrow and John Dillinger are folk heroes to a lot of people to this day. Their brutal crimes against innocent people are set aside in favor of a romantic ideal of independence and sticking it to the man.

It took this country several decades to figure out how to put an end to organized crime or at least to minimize it. The RICO Act (Racketeer Influenced and Corrupt Organizations Act) was passed in 1970 finally giving law enforcement the tools it needed to combat organized crime. This one act has all but put an end to organized crime and organizations like the Mafia and the Hells Angels Motorcycle Club. Even some police departments, Major League Baseball and some other government organizations have fallen to the RICO Act.

Most of us who live in the U.S. take our safety for granted. It hasn't always been that way. In fact, I would say that the second half of the 20th century up until present times are the safest anyone has ever experienced. It is getting less safe. School shootings have become common, some of our cities are falling into chaos and crime in general is on the rise.

Unfortunately, I believe that since 2020 our cities have fallen back into a culture of crime. The institutions we depend on to protect us have deteriorated along with our cities. This creates an atmosphere of tolerance of crime and a confusion that leaves the door open for people who are determined to commit crimes. It distracts our resources from being able to pursue crimes in places like Colorado City, Arizona and Hildale, Utah. We're too busy gathering up criminals who have been allowed to cross our borders to deal with American citizens who are trafficking and raping underage girls and boys.

If you're reading this and are offended by my reference to what is happening in our country, please try to stay focused on my point. Whether you believe in open borders, the rights of criminals, or whatever, you have to admit that these things are competing with our ability to protect innocent children. And that's the only point I'm making.

If you doubt the things I am writing or think it's not still happening, check out this Amber Alert that I just happened to receive on my phone as I'm writing, and the associated article that came up in my email:

Amber Alert for Allen and Rachelle Fischer.

On June 22 Jefferson County Sheriff's Office received a report of two missing juveniles from Monteview. Allen Larand Fisher, 13 and Rachelle Leray Fischer, 15 are believed to have left Monteview to return to Trenton Utah, where they previously lived. The children are possibly traveling in a gray Honda or Hyundai sedan with Utah license plates. Allen is 5'9", 135 pounds with longer sandy blonde hair and blue eyes. Racheal is 5'5", 135 pounds with brown hair and blue eyes.

We... See more

👍 3   💬 1   ➤ 20

Police were notified in June, 2025. Where are they now? Article by Nate Eaton, KTVB7

Fortunately, there are good people who are fighting the fight to expose what is happening. People like Mike Watkiss, a long-time reporter who has written a lot about Warren Jeffs, his crimes and his victims. Mike has a ton of knowledge and a deep interest in what has happened in Colorado City and what is still happening. Nate Eaton who never let the question of "where are the kids?" in the LVD and Chad Daybell case drop. Nate has been relentless in his coverage of our case.

I have had the privilege of spending time with both of these men and many other people in the media and they give me hope that real journalism is alive and well. You just don't find it on cable or network news anymore. In fact, a lot of the journalists who are covering this case are refugees from cable and network news.

I am proud to be associated in my small way with everyone who is working to expose the corruption and crime that has infiltrated some of our communities. Unfortunately, it takes time to make change and bring people like Warren Jeffs to justice and not all of them ever see justice. However, I believe the people committing crimes against children will have their day of reckoning.

I recently spent some time in Colorado City and Hildale. You may have heard of it or read something about it. You may have heard its original name: Short Creek or The Crick, still used by a lot of the people who live there. It's difficult for me to believe that a place like this exists in our country and I had to see it for myself.

The towns sit in a beautiful and exotic location at the base of Zion National Park. It is surrounded by tall red cliffs. It was founded in 1913 by members of The Council of Friends in order for them to continue the practice of polygamy without being bothered by the outside world. The Council of Friends was originally run by a board of 7 members. It started out as part of the Mormon Church, but was officially excommunicated in 1935 after refusing to give up polygamy. John Barlow was the prophet at the time. Barlow had five wives. A small number for a prophet of the FLDS.

Colorado City and Hildale. Personal photo.

When Rulon Jeffs came to power in the 1950s the board began to deteriorate as he took on more power on his own. In the 1990s his son Warren Jeffs continued that until his control was total.

Following the death of his father, Jeffs became a dictator, dictating all aspects of people's lives including what colors they could and could not wear. Warren even took his father's many wives as his own. So, women who had been mothers to him were now his wives.

Further, Jeffs took control over the UEP (United Effort Plan) a corporation owned by the FLDS which owned all of the land in Colorado City and Hildale. He confiscated that land out from under the people who lived on it and had built their houses on it whenever he decided it was to his benefit to do so. He rewrote church doctrine in order to gain total control and seek perfect obedience from his flock. The internet, toys, bikes, holidays, newspapers, books and more were eventually banned. He ordered the marriages of underage girls to old men. The families of these underage girls had no say in the matter. A lot of them supported Jeffs and thought that marrying their adolescent daughters to men with high standing was a good thing.

"Apostates" (people who left the church or were excommunicated) were banned from the community and thought to be worse than the gentiles (anyone not a member of the FLDS). Jeffs even controlled the water and power that supplied people's homes and would have it turned off if he thought the people living in those homes were not complying to the level he required. He ran the police department like his own gestapo force. People were terrified to testify or even talk about the crimes that were committed against them or their families. If they did talk, the price they would pay would be high.

People who weren't in Warren Jeffs' favor were often sent off to remote properties owned by the UEP to live alone away from their families and even their young children, often for years at a time. These places were given numbers denoting how long it took to drive there from Short Creek. For instance, R17(Refuge 17) in Colorado was a 17-hour drive. R23 in South Dakota was a 23-hour drive.

Jeffs required people to admit to the infractions they didn't commit. If they did repent enough and admit to their supposed errors or infractions, they might be rebaptized into the church. It was up to the whims of Jeffs. That made it extremely difficult for anyone trying to bring Jeffs to justice and stop him from committing his obvious crimes against the most innocent people. Those who were kicked out of their homes and forced to leave the community still had family living there and Jeffs threatened to harm them if anyone talked to authorities. Jeffs "owned" the police so it was impossible to protect people living in The Crick. People who chose to leave the church and the community of their own free will were considered the most wicked of all.

It seemed that the more people on the outside tried to expose Jeffs and his crimes, the more support he got from his "followers". Eventually with mounting pressure, cracks began to appear and some people finally had the nerve to make a stand against Jeffs, spelling the end of Jeffs' stranglehold on the towns. Some of the "apostates" who he had expelled from his community taking everything they owned, including their families, finally took the risk of offending him further and testified to a grand jury against Jeffs.

The problems run deep and are extremely hard to solve. There exists a sorority of wives who help to recruit the younger females. There is "groupthink". Anyone going against the opinion of the group is chastised or unwelcome. There is an extreme form of cognitive dissonance. People are motivated to solve their conflicts between what they know to be right and what they are told to believe, by simply believing the thing they are told. It lessens the tension and allows people to live with themselves.

If you love and believe in someone you are not going to believe in the things you see them doing that are wrong. You are going to convince yourself that the wrong things are actually right. Especially if you have invested your whole life into the people you follow, the house you built, the community you have supported and even the old man you handed your daughter over to. You have made huge sacrifices and don't want to lose your investment. If you are a young girl, you probably grew up being taught to hope to marry the prophet. As a father you may have given your wives and daughters to the prophet. You can't imagine or ever admit to yourself that you did these things in vain or subjugated yourself and your family to a common predator.

The location of Short Creek was chosen because of its remoteness and inaccessibility. It's an interesting set up really. Colorado City is in AZ and Hildale is in UT. But really, they are the same city. The only visible separation is a sign on the highway. There is an obvious advantage to being on the border between two states. If the police in AZ are after you, you just have to hop over to your friend or relative's house across the border in Utah and vice versa. It just makes it more complicated and time consuming for the police.

The community has gone through some changes since their leader, Warren Jeffs, was arrested by the FBI and eventually sentenced to life in prison for his crimes against women and children. My wife and I were on our way to Lori Vallow Daybell's trial in Phoenix when we took a detour into the depths of what is commonly called the Arizona Strip to see firsthand what Colorado City and Hildale are like today. We were surprised to find a coffee shop and decided to go in to see what it was like. I can tell you that the whole town seemed weird and so did the coffee shop. Maybe it was just our preconceived notion of it all, but everything seemed a little off.

The question that came to both of our minds was: Is this coffee shop the fundamentalist Mormons bleeding the beast? Were they fundamentalists selling coffee to the gentiles? It sure looked that way. I don't mean to make light of what people living there are trying to do. It's been an uphill battle to save the community and turn it from a literal hell hole into a thriving free community.

I've read a lot about outsiders' experiences there in the past. We were not followed around town by lifted four-wheel drive pickups with tinted windows, but we did see a fleet of them parked by the police station. The most striking thing we saw were the huge sprawling houses and dirty yards and streets. The houses looked more like compounds really. Bare plywood walls. Nothing seemed completed. Very few had any grass or any landscaping at all. Just a lot of bare dirt. There were some very nice homes with well-kept yards, but the majority looked barely livable by today's standards. It reminded me of some of the reservations I have visited except here the houses were so big. It definitely looked like a place where people's freedom was given or taken away by someone or something.

Just a few of many such houses in Colorado City. Personal photo.

The community has been controversial since its founding. The fundamentalist Mormons who chose to live there hoped to live in peace, free to practice their religion without interference. But, in 1953 the governor of AZ, John H. Pyle sent the National Guard into the area in an attempt to stop polygamy and its associated crimes. Everyone living in Short Creek was arrested including children. The children were taken from their parents. Some of the parents never regained custody of their children. The raid received a huge amount of press coverage and ended with Pyle losing his political standing and his governorship.

Because of the political and public relations backlash, it wasn't until 50 years later that someone was finally held to account for unlawful sexual conduct with a minor. Short Creek police officer Rodney Holm was convicted for impregnating his sixteen-year-old plural wife, Ruth Stubbs.

Shortly after that the Yearning For Zion Ranch in Eldorado Texas was raided, sparking another public relations nightmare. (I write more about the raid in *Chad Daybell, The One Mighty and Strong)*

In 2004 the leader of the Fundamentalist Church of Jesus Christ of Latter-day Saints, Warren Jeffs ordered the expulsion from the church and the community of 20 prominent men. He gave their wives and children to other men who happened to be in his favor at the time. He was also responsible for what is known as the lost boys. Young men coming of age were in competition with the older men for the young women and girls. There just weren't enough women and girls to go around, so Jeffs had a lot of the young men and boys tossed out of the community for the smallest infractions of his rules. Most ended up in the close-by communities of Hurricane, St. George and Salt Lake City, struggling to survive on their own in a world they knew nothing about and had been taught to fear.

In May 2006 Jeffs was placed on the FBI Ten Most Wanted List. There was evidence of him sexually abusing boys in Alta Academy (the local church run elementary school) and trafficking girls and young women among other crimes.

The school is also where according to Rachel Jeffs, Warren's daughter, who has since escaped Jeffs and the FLDS, in her book, *Breaking Free*, he would call her into his office and force her to touch him inappropriately while he did the same to her. He later told her he was testing her. I suppose in his twisted mind, to see if she was worthy.

Also, according to Rachel, he started showing her pornography when she was just ten years old. When she later confronted him about it his response was:

"You should be grateful that you are part of the priesthood."

As all girls did in the FLDS, Rachel quit school after 8th grade. It wasn't thought that women needed any higher education in order to serve their husbands.

Jeffs roamed free in an expensive SUV caravan exploring the country while avoiding arrest. He was known to have been at Mardi Gras in Louisiana and other locations that he himself would not have approved of. There are pictures of him wearing shorts which was a big violation of his own rules. He required the men and boys in his community to wear long sleeve shirts buttoned to the neck. Shorts or the showing of any unnecessary skin was absolutely not allowed.

On August 8, 2006 he was finally arrested and eventually sentenced to life in prison. In spite of all of the evidence against him and his obvious crimes in his community, many people continued to follow him, receiving long messages and in-depth directions from him from prison. In 2011, 2,000 members of the FLDS voted unanimously to uphold Jeffs' authority. When Willie Jessop, Jeffs' supposed successor, opposed Jeffs, he was declared an apostate and kicked out of the church.

Somehow Jeffs still has a strong influence in the community and a strong following even from his prison cell. He puts out revelations through proxies and there are many who follow his directions. They still believe that Jesus speaks through him and that he is a martyr.

The UEP (United Effort Plan) no longer owns the land the houses sit on. The UEP is a business entity owned by the FLDS. In 2005 a Utah court took the land away from the UEP and put it in a trust for the people who built the houses that sat on it. To this day though there are ongoing land disputes between the people who spent their own money and labor to build their homes and the UEP.

The elementary school where Jeffs was the superintendent and routinely committed his crimes against young boys and girls is still standing, but empty. It has been replaced by a modern building and grounds that are hopefully being run by reasonable people.

UEP still prominent. Personal photo.

The old elementary school was abandoned after Jeff's arrest.
Personal photo.

New modern High School. Personal photo.

I couldn't find the UEP headquarters where Jeffs was known to rule the community from. I think the building has been erased from the community. Certainly, the high fence and cameras that surrounded it are gone.

Members of the FLDS who lived there are mostly scattered to the winds although some still live there and practice polygamy. The ones who left are in remote places in Idaho, Nebraska, Minnesota and elsewhere doing their best to hide their past and their unlawful lifestyle.

Driving around Colorado City and Hildale, we stumbled upon Cottonwood Park. It looked like a wonderful community park where families could gather and kids could play. It even has a narrow-gauge railway winding around it although I didn't see any sign of a train. Everywhere though one is reminded of where one is. In the park we saw a stone monument commemorating the siege that took place in 1953.

Beautiful backdrop for a park. Personal photo.

Monument commemorating the words of Uncle Roy.
Personal photo.

After the successful arrest and conviction of Jeffs, several other prominent men in the FLDS have been convicted of offenses relating to marrying underage girls. I don't think it has put a stop to it though. It has chased those who feed off of young women and girls further underground. There are still plenty of people who have utter faith in a convicted pedophile.

The point of this chapter is to give the reader a feel for the fundamentalist roots that run deep in Utah, Arizona and Southern Idaho. Those roots are what gave rise to current groups that have sprouted up around the area in recent times. The origins of the roots are a mistrust of the federal government, religious beliefs that are outside of the mainstream Mormon Church or any mainstream church, an ignorance of current events, a belief that the second coming of Christ is happening soon, ignorance of our history and our culture and a stubbornness and arrogance born from all of those things.

The FLDS and other offshoots of the Mormon Church still exist and in fact are gaining strength. There are also many groups that don't claim to be a church of their own, but do claim to have answers that the church won't give. Groups like AVOW and Preparing a People. There are more, but these are the ones Chad was associated with. There are individuals like Chad Daybell who claim to have answers beyond what the church can give. Energy healers and near-death experience claimants. People who claim to have a heightened religious standing. People who claim to have the voice of God or angels in their head. The only difference I can see between Warren Jeffs and Chad Daybell is that Jeffs is at least ten times smarter than Daybell. Daybell was doing his best to follow in the footsteps of several people, using the manipulative ideas he learned from them.

In August 2022 Warren Jeffs published a revelation through his wife; Merilyn S. Jeffs, his sister, Rachel Jeffs, and his son or possibly nephew, Helaman Jeffs. It reads in part (It's over ten pages long so I will give you the "high" points):

"To all who receive this testimony letter of I, Merilyn Steed Jeffs, appointed by Jesus Christ through Keyholder Warren Steed Jeffs..."
(Apparently his wife, Marilyn and others are able to meet with Jeffs in prison and write down his revelations)

"His servant Warren Jeffs, His mortal Keyholder on earth at this time, as he speaks the very words of Jesus Christ in revelations and teachings given His people..."
(Here Jeffs is saying that Jesus speaks directly through him)

"...and to be protected against the thrusts of the evil powers which are increasingly seeking to stop the progression of the work of God, but they will fail to do so."
(He's talking about the police, politicians and the rest of us trying to stop him from committing his crimes)

"I know the Lord is blessing us beyond measure, to receive His holy eternity truths revealed through his Prophet..."
(His followers are so lucky to have a Jeffs)

"...to live in Celestial oneness powers with His will through His Prophet..."
"...to be numbered among His Zion pure Israel elect..."
(Jeffs' way of speaking is sometimes obscure, but what he means in the above two passages is that through

perfect obedience to him, one can be worthy of the Celestial Kingdom)

"The One Man we all look to, as the Example of how we should be...the Lord does lead and guide Him right..."
(Jeffs is the example of how we all should be!)

"I, Jesus Christ, give mine own word through my Key-holder on earth, Warren Steed Jeffs, sacred council..."
(According to Jeffs, Jesus is literally speaking through him)

"Receive my word in any typed, approved by Key-holder on earth, Warren Jeffs sermons...his sermons as doctrine, revelations of Jesus Christ...Jesus Christ appointing him to prepare them..."
(When one of Jeffs' proxies speaks, it is the word of Jesus through Jeffs, through the proxy and it still holds the same weight)

"And before you are resurrected to the highest degree of glory, you must prove you will constantly live in the increase of the Spirit of God in greater and increasing degrees."
(His followers are going to have to try harder to prove themselves worthy)

"And the God-office men angels resurrected to the highest degree of glory are called each a 'God in His Own Right', a "God of Creation".
(Here he is saying that worthy men will become gods of their own creation. IE: they will have their own planet)

"...on this mortal telestial probationary world..."
(We have heard the same words from Chad Daybell)

"You must not partake of the television, or the gentile music, or use the internet and its terrible immoral murderous display of the sins of this most wicked generation that has ever inhabited this world."
(He has to keep his flock ignorant or they will know better than to follow a lunatic)

"I, the Lord Jesus Christ, am causing my servant Warren Steed Jeffs, my Keyholder on Earth, to teach train saints of Jesus Christ how to dwell in Celestial oneness with Heavenly Father..."
(He is the one Jesus picked to teach people how to be worthy of Heaven. Read on and we see what he means by that)

"And I, the Lord, give you a sacred revealing as part of the sacred keeping to your souls."
(He is saying he is about to reveal something important)

"...that less than five and one-half years from now date, of the gentile calendar..."
(something big is going to happen 5-½ years from August 8, 2022)

"And the New Jerusalem Zion City prophesied to be built on North America continent, the Center Stake of Jackson County, Missouri, will soon begin after the sudden-striking full-cleansing soon-sent whirlwind judgements of Jesus Christ depopulate both North and South America of all wicked people and wicked nation.

And the righteous saints will be lifted up and be placed in hidden United Order communities..."
(he's talking about the second coming of Christ and the cleansing or killing of all of those who aren't worthy. I wonder if Chad read this)

"And they will prepare themselves and their children to either be translated or Celestial resurrected..."
(This is the main point of Jeffs' prophecy. He is telling his flock to prepare to die so they can make it to heaven. Also, prepare their children to die. Remember Jim Jones. In Guyana he convinced his followers to drink a cyanide laced drink and force their children to drink it)

(Jeffs goes on to talk about the degrees one can reach in the Celestial Kingdom. If you don't have enough wives and children, but are pure enough, you can live for a while in Heaven. Better get busy. Those who are unworthy will be on a different planet. Men and women separated on their own planets)

(According to Jeffs, negroes and dark-skinned people who have corrupted the white man's world have no chance)

"...earn the highest degree of glory in the Celestial Kingdom, through think-praying, prayer first, praying always instant by instant..."
(He says the second half of that sentence over and over. A method of brain-washing)

"I, the Lord, loveth all. Receive this with gladness."
(He is saying his followers should be happy they are
about to die and go to Heaven)

"…because translated people must die…And translated
people must die."
(He is making it clear that his followers must die in
order to make it to the Celestial Kingdom. He clearly
gives the date and says they must die)

Well, that's pretty clear. Okay, that was a little hard to get
through and I didn't make you read the whole thing. I know
it's hard to interpret what he is saying. It's pure brainwashing.
Saying things over and over until the words are in someone's
head like a bad song you can't quit playing in your mind. Chad
used the same monotone voice in his blessings and a lot of the
same words and phrases.

Just to be clear, one could say that in taking only a few
passages out of the ten pages of Jeffs' revelation, I could be
taking it out of context in order to make a point. I will tell
you that if anything is out of context, I make it sound less
threatening and not more threatening. It's just that anything
Jeffs says is wordy and monotonous. It took him ten pages to
make a simple point here. Simple yes, but also terrifying. 5-½
years from August 8, 2022 would be January 8, 2028. I hope we
can keep him from convincing his followers from committing
suicide on themselves and murder on their children.

And, even though it's monotonous and wordy, Jeffs means
everything he says. He has always followed through when he
can convince his flock to go along with him. Like Lori Vallow
Daybell, Jeffs has no feeling or human emotion. He is incapa-
ble of feeling remorse, compassion or sympathy for even the
most vulnerable among us. He has hurt people terribly both

emotionally and physically and he could care less. He has destroyed families, stolen what is rightfully theirs and raped young girls and boys mercilessly. And this is supposedly his flock. When we think of someone's flock, we think of defenseless sheep cared for by a sheepherder. If Jeffs' followers are sheep and Jeffs is a sheepherder, he is a sheepherder from hell. Or maybe a wolf in sheep's clothing.

4

DISPERSE
TO THE WINDS

In December, 2024 Sam Bateman was sentenced to 50 years in prison for Conspiracy to Commit Transportation of a Minor for Criminal Sexual Activity and Conspiracy to Commit Kidnapping. He had a network that encompassed four states. He was the leader of a sex trafficking ring that primarily trafficked underage girls for the purpose of marrying them off to older men. Upon his arrest, Bateman's co-conspirators scattered. Some of them have been indicted and as far as I can tell some are still living free. Some of the parents of the children who were being raped, trafficked and married off to older men lied for Bateman to protect him. These parents were given the opportunity to protect their children and make Bateman pay for his abuses, but they chose instead to protect him.

Bateman's followers willingly gave over their daughters even though they knew they were to be forced to "marry" older men not of their choosing and that they would most likely never see their daughters again. The youngest was only nine years old. In court it was shown that Bateman forced these young girls to have group sex with him and others. The young girls were told it was their religious duty to have sex with the men and that their very salvation was at stake. Bateman was finally arrested in 2022.

The FLDS owned a motel deep in the Nevada desert north of Las Vegas called the Caliente Hot Springs Motel. Between 1997 and 2004 dozens of "marriages" were performed in room 15. Room 15 was a bleak, plain, outdated motel room. Not a happy place, but a place where the lives, as they knew it, of the girls brought there were ended. On some weekends of marriages as many as ten would take place, usually with the father and his trusted plural wives in attendance. When the ceremony ended the older men would take their child "brides" to another room to consummate the "marriage" while the families shared a meal together to celebrate.

In 2003 the state of Utah started to prosecute for Bigamy and underage sex putting pressure on Bateman. In the judge's statement at Bateman's sentencing, she said:

"You took them from their homes, their families and made them into sex slaves. You stripped them of their innocence and childhood."

He very surely did all of that, but I'm not sure if she addressed the depth of the problem. The families she talks about gave their daughters to Bateman willingly. They thought that by sacrificing their daughters they would raise their own standing in the FLDS. The fathers and mothers knew very well what was going to happen to their underage daughters. They gave them up to bondage sexually, spiritually and in every way imaginable.

Even behind bars these patriarchs wield power. They are so wrapped up in their own power that they continue to disrupt the lives of their followers. Evil men like Bateman and Jeffs are as dangerous in prison as they are out. They get some kind of satisfaction out of it even though they have no physical contact. From his prison cell in Arizona, Bateman orchestrated the kidnapping of eight underage girls who later went on to testify against him in Federal Court.

5

FREEDOM OF THE PRESS

The framers of our constitution knew at its inception that our constitution was imperfect and incomplete, so they provided for amendments. The First Amendment, the "Bill of Rights" covers religious freedoms, free speech, freedom of the press, the right to peaceful protest and the right to petition the government. This one bill made our country the only country in history to provide those rights to its citizens.

Thomas Jefferson knew it was imperfect. Freedom of the press meant that anyone with a printing press could distribute information, true or false about whatever they chose. But he also knew that this one amendment would give more power to the people of our country over the government than any other provision.

It has been abused by many people in the media since its inception. Reporting the truth and the complete story has very often been replaced by propaganda and outright lies. The motivation for doing this is sometimes an attempt to sway voters to vote a certain way. Sometimes it's to gain sympathy for an individual or an institution. Too often it's a way for a reporter or media outlet to gain fame and fortune.

The reporting of the FLDS has been varied and oftentimes flawed. Public opinion based on the reporting of what was happening in Colorado City, Utah and the YFZ (Yearning For Zion) Ranch in Texas was influenced primarily by what people saw on TV.

The Oprah Winfrey Show was wildly popular during the time of the raid on the YFZ Ranch and most people who had no idea before Oprah's coverage about the FLDS, Warren Jeffs or that polygamy even existed in our country, got their information from her. Undoubtedly, her coverage of what was going on at the YFZ Ranch and what life was like for the people who lived there, influenced the course of events.

Oprah's coverage comes off now as naive, but I think she knew what was actually going on there. Her coverage shows people who are strange to the rest of us, but happily living their lives the way they chose. Polygamist families that may not be perfect, that might be ignorant of events in the outside world, but who have freely made a choice to live a simple life of peace and happiness. Kind of like the Amish. Different and set apart by their own choice. One could almost be envious.

The truth was that the people living at the YFZ Ranch were the worst of the worst of the FLDS. They were the ones in Warren Jeffs' favor. They were the ones who took other men's wives and families when Jeffs stole them and banished the father from the community. They were the ones who willingly handed over their young daughters to older men. They were the ones who would lie for Jeffs and cover his crimes no matter what the cost. And they were the ones who were good at it.

The children were so conditioned that most of them believed the things they said in answer to Oprah's questions. Even if they questioned those things, they were positive that those things were right. The questioning of those things must be a fault of their own. I'm absolutely positive though, that there were at least a few of those kids who were terrified to speak their truth. There was always a high price to pay for those who went against the hierarchy.

Oprah covered for herself by asking the hard questions, but she knew the answers she got were lies and she knew that her coverage would influence public opinion to support the people living at the YFZ Ranch and their way of life.

We know their way of life was not the ideal that we saw on her show. We know that underage girls were being married off to old men. We know that immediately following the "marriage" ceremony they were taken to a room behind the altar and raped while others kneeled around the bed and watched.

I know what life was like for the women and children living there because I watched true reporting from people like Mike Watkiss. They had no choice. No choice in who they married and when they would marry, no choice in how many children they would bear and take care of, no choice in how many hours they labored, no choice in what or who they worshipped, no choice in at what age they would have to serve the men in the bedroom and no choice in whether they lived there or not.

Men and boys were forced to work 22 hours a day, seven days a week in order to meet Jeffs' impossible deadlines. If they failed to meet those deadlines they were sent off to live in exile in places like R17 or R23 if they were lucky. If they weren't so lucky they were declared apostates and sent off to find their way in the world on their own, with no contact with anyone including their own fathers and mothers. Jeffs called them "Laborers of Zion". They understood that they always had that threat over their heads so they slaved away, depriving themselves of sleep and the food they needed.

Very simply, the women and children were slaves to the men in every way imaginable. Boys were somehow allowed to work like dogs for FLDS owned construction companies doing projects all over the country, but especially in Henderson and Las Vegas, Nevada. Jeffs had received a "revelation" he called the "New Law of Sarah". It allowed him to have multiple wives, some of whom were underage, with him in a bedroom where they were to sexually excite and touch each other. He said this was in order to alleviate the stress he was under because he was responsible and had to atone for his followers' sins. Jeffs seemed to get pleasure from the "wives" disgust at what he forced them to do. They were all slaves even to the point where they were terrified to tell the truth to someone like Oprah. So, public opinion was formed by Oprah's reporting.

Unfortunately, public opinion led to the raid on the YFZ Ranch being in most ways a failure. The children who had been rescued by the Texas Rangers and Child Protective Services from a life of brainwashing, slavery and sexual abuse perpetrated by Warren Jeffs through the hierarchy down to their parents, were eventually handed back to Jeffs, the hierarchy and the parents, because of pressure from the public who had a skewed view of what was happening there. People thought that the religious rights of members of the FLDS were being infringed upon by an overzealous government. The public had no real idea of the horrors the members were suffering.

Fortunately, there were a few who spoke out in spite of the danger and the loss that came with daring to go against what had proven to be a very powerful, but small group of men who held more power than anyone has a right to.

Warren Jeffs' own daughter Rachel recently spoke out on Megyn Kelly's podcast about how Jeffs began raping her when she was 8 years old. How he constantly exposed her to pornography. As an adult she spoke out, knowing it put her in imminent danger and that she would lose her family, her friends and the only life she ever knew. She is one of the few who could see through the brainwashing and was willing to speak out in order to save others from what she had suffered.

So, here we are still in a place in the U.S. where we allow this to go on. But, what does all of this have to do with Chad and LVD? Remember, my premise is that we created Chad and LVD. Our public opinion, having been swayed by misinformation, led by our deep desire to live our lives in the way we choose, created a space for Chad and LVD to exist.

When I sat as a juror in LVD's trial in Idaho, I was shocked by a lot of what I was hearing. Not just the horrible brutality, but also by the terminology I was hearing. I had some knowledge about the FLDS, Mountain Meadows, the history of the Mormon Church and our country's history in general. What shocked me, is that I found myself in the middle of a trial that as it progressed, was proving to be closely tied to the fundamentalist beliefs or proclaimed beliefs of people like Warren Jeffs. I knew that most people hadn't studied it all like I had and I wondered if my fellow jurors, the police, the prosecutors and even the judge realized the enormity of the problem. I wondered if they realized that the trial we were a part of was just one piece of a larger puzzle.

This is why I decided I needed to write my books. I had to make a choice. I had thought that our duty as jurors was to serve our time and then go back to our lives. Not make it about ourselves. It's just our duty as citizens. We do it quietly and move on. If we bring attention to ourselves, it must be for selfish purposes.

But people need to know the enormity of the problem. They need to know that Chad and LVD didn't exist in their own crazy world with a few stupid followers. It's a bigger world that they existed in and the problems are bigger than just this case.

As far as I know Oprah has never apologized or made up for her at the least incomplete reporting. She is one of the richest women in the world with her own network, making her money on reporting on things like the FLDS, gaining a massive following from it. She certainly could have done it. When the truth did come out thanks to real journalism, she could have done a show showing the truth. The question I'm left with is why didn't she?

When Jeffs was finally arrested for some of his crimes he was placed in Purgatory Correctional Facility in St. George, Utah for a year while he awaited his trial. Being held in isolation, he repeatedly tried to hurt himself and even attempted to commit suicide. He also denounced himself as prophet and confessed to being immoral. He later recanted his statements through his attorneys. Jeffs is currently serving life in prison in Texas for sexually assaulting minor girls. He still controls every aspect of many people's lives.

In court in Texas Jeffs represented himself much like Lori Vallow Daybell almost 20 years later. I was watching LVD closely expecting that at some point she would follow further in Jeffs' footsteps and give revelations in court. She didn't do that although she got close a few times. Judge Beresky was good at calling for a break when it looked like she was about to go down that road. In the end what convicted Jeffs was his own recordings and DNA evidence. It took the jury only four hours to convict. At the time of his conviction Jeffs had 78 wives, one third of whom were underage.

Following his conviction Jeffs ordered his followers to give over all of their personal possessions to the church. He restricted married people from having any kind of sexual relations or even hugging each other. Miscarriages or condoms were acts of murder. For one to touch their own privates for any reason was a sin. This created a condition within the FLDS that was unbearable for most. Some people even went crazy. It also created a space that needed to be filled and I believe led to Sam Bateman and his horrible crimes.

I mentioned Mike Watkiss earlier. He is a retired journalist who had covered the truth about the FLDS in depth as it was happening. He spent a lot of time in Colorado City making a nuisance of himself with the powers that existed there. Because of a lack of honest reporting and I think because of changes in the way news is disseminated, he has thankfully come out of retirement and is again reporting on what is really going on. It's thanks to people like him and more than a few podcasters that we have any truth at all about who people like Warren Jeffs really are.

According to Watkiss he was uncomfortably happy being a retired journalist. He was burnt out from decades of covering Warren Jeffs. He had done what he could and was doing his best to be okay with leaving it at that.

What happened next when he least expected it, like important things in our lives tend to do, drug him right back in. I get my information for the rest of this chapter from his interview with Lauren Matthias and her *Hidden True Crime Podcast* among other places.

Watkiss said that none of the events surrounding fundamentalism are isolated. This supports my personal belief that Chad and LVD, Warren Jeffs, Sam Bateman and many others are part of an organized network. Even though Colorado City and Hildale have been forced to change and even though the FLDS was forced to "scatter" after the arrest of Jeffs, there is still an organized crime network feeding on young children that is run primarily by Jeffs from his prison cell.

Watkiss goes on to say (and I agree with him wholeheartedly) that there needs to be more of a sense of urgency in dealing with the FLDS. Their crimes are too horrible and continuous for us to just sit back and wait for law enforcement to finally do something about it.

So, what brought Mike Watkiss back into seeking justice? In December, 2021 out of the blue and totally unexpectedly, Watkiss received a call from Sam Bateman himself asking to meet in person. Watkiss had been on Jeffs' "hit list" for years and he was suspicious of why Bateman would want to meet with him. After thinking about it for several days, he decided it would be safer to meet with Bateman than to wait until Bateman found him. Better for Watkiss to meet Bateman on his own terms at a place of his own choosing.

When they finally met, Bateman had a van full of wives who he introduced as his ladies, some of whom were obviously under age, with him. He had his wives sing songs to Watkiss. Watkiss was confused, but went along with it while he had his son-in-law video the whole encounter. Watkiss had a plan to hand over the video to the FBI thinking they would use it to arrest Bateman. Watkiss had had a good working relationship with the FBI in his pursuit of the FLDS and had even been awarded a medal for his service.

Nothing happened. Bateman was running free. Days, weeks and months passed. The evidence Watkiss and others had gathered against Bateman was horrific. He was raping underage girls up to four times a day. He was holding them in bondage. He was making pornographic movies with them and sharing the movies with his associates. There were recorded phone conversations alluding to these things.

Finally, during a routine traffic stop in August, 2022, an Arizona trooper noticed something suspicious. Bateman had a box trailer with three young girls inside. The trooper noticed a little hand sticking out of the slats and he noticed a wedding ring on the little finger. Because of the information gathered by Watkiss and others, the police were aware of Bateman and his crimes and this was an easy opportunity to finally arrest him. Bateman got caught not because of good police work, but because he was stupid.

According to prosecutors, Bateman organized "sacred ordinances" where he would allow other men to rape his underage "wives" while he watched. He treated them like chattel and controlled every aspect of their lives. He traded them with other men and took them back as he pleased. He destroyed these young girls' lives.

Watkiss attended Bateman's trial and says it's a good thing the courtroom was full of police. He thinks without that some jurors would have come at and killed Bateman on the spot. The evidence the jurors were exposed to was that horrific. I can relate.

Prior to his arrest Bateman was a revered member of the FLDS. People even gifted him an expensive Bently automobile among other things. The worst gifts he received, of course, were given to him by fathers of underage girls and those fathers did it willingly.

I think there are so many problems with the FLDS that I can't even count them. All of the problems though, have their roots in the same source. The original Mormon doctrine and the idea that one man can have the voice of God speak through him. That gives that one man absolute power, the ability to brainwash and the ability to abuse that power to whatever evil extreme that one man desires. Bateman had declared himself to be the prophet with the voice of God in his head and unfortunately some people believed him.

In spite of my prior interest in the history of our country and all of the violence that it includes, before I sat as a juror in the Lori Vallow Daybell trial, I would have had a hard time believing that a Warren Jeffs, Sam Bateman, Chad Daybell or Lori Vallow Daybell could exist. I knew of Jeffs, had read a lot about him and his crimes, but none of it became real to me until I was confronted with it literally face to face.

Only now do I understand how important it is that we put our own wants and comfortable lives aside in the pursuit to help these helpless children. Only now do I understand the danger they are in. Only now do I understand the enormity of our failure to save them from these monsters who look us in the eye and claim to be good people, while in reality they are abusing, raping, enslaving and murdering our children. We know who they are. Do we see them yet? For what they really are? We're about to find out.

Elizabeth Roundy's children have been abducted by these people. We are aware of it. What will we do? I'm already hearing how hard it will be to find these two underage kids who have been kidnapped for the purpose of raping them and possibly for convincing them to commit suicide in 2028. I'm not buying it. I think it just shows an unwillingness on the part of law enforcement to do the hard work. We can find a terrorist leader deep in a cave in the heart of the middle eastern desert. Surely, we can find these children. We just need the political will to do it.

The last reporting I can find was from July 19, 2025 and it was just a repeat of Elizabeth Roundy's interview taken right after the kids were kidnapped. As I write this, it's late September. These kids have been missing for over three months. That's terrifying, but what's more terrifying to me is that it seems to me that we have forgotten them, just written them off to whatever their fate is.

6

IS IT TERRORISM?

So, are groups like the FLDS terrorists? The definition of domestic terrorism is: The use of violence and intimidation, often against civilians, to achieve political or social aims.

Violence and intimidation are defined as: Terrorism relies on acts of violence or the threat of violence to instill fear and panic.

Political or social aims are defined as: influencing government policy or promoting a particular ideology.

The answer is certainly yes. The FLDS does all of the things listed above and more. We can throw in intimidation of minors, intimidation of families and a lot more.

In her book, Rachel Jeffs says that when she watched a documentary about Osama bin Laden, his ability to brainwash his followers and get them to do his bidding, reminded her of her father.

Why is our government hesitant then to call Warren Jeffs and the FLDS a terrorist organization? It would open up a lot of possibilities for the weapons we could use to save children like Allen and Rachelle Fischer.

I think reading this book gives us the answer. Starting with the Mountain Meadows massacre and going through the failed raids on the FLDS in Texas. Also, consider what happened in Waco, TX in 1993 and the raid on Randall Weaver and his family in Ruby Ridge, Idaho in 1992.

In Ruby Ridge federal law enforcement officers attempted to arrest Weaver on weapons charges. The Weaver family holed up in their cabin in Northern Idaho on property they owned. Weaver's wife and son were killed by federal officers. A U.S. Marshal was also killed. Weaver was eventually arrested, but later acquitted of most of the charges against him. The Weaver family sued the Federal Government and won a $3.1 million dollar lawsuit. Of course, this standoff resulted in a lot of anti-government sentiment. Since this standoff, and other almost equally failed attempts by the government to hold people who live outside the norm accountable, federal law enforcement agencies have changed the way they approach situations like Ruby Ridge.

Public opinion has a way of turning on government officials when they use their powers on American citizens. Especially for "sex crimes". What is a sex crime? Certainly, Warren Jeffs is guilty of sex crimes. A huge majority of people in the U.S. would agree that forcing underage girls or boys to have sex is a crime. Forcing women or anyone to have sex is a sex crime. Trafficking women and children in order to marry them off to men they don't have a choice in marrying is a sex crime.

But look at the trial of Shawn Diddy Combs. I think it shows where we are in our country in how we think about sex and what is and what is not okay. I think the prosecutors underestimated our tolerance for what is and what is not okay. We're okay with "freak offs". We really just don't care what grown adults willingly do. If adults want to do a lot of drugs and have all kinds of sex with any number of people, we don't care. Maybe it's not for us, but who are we to tell someone else how to live their life.

Of course there are many people who support Combs because of his stature. They would love him no matter what he did. They would love him if he beat women. They would love him if he forced them to do drugs so they could commit sex acts they wouldn't do sober. That's not what I'm talking about. What I'm saying is that we just no longer have the will to judge others for doing things that aren't hurting anyone. You can make the argument that he is hurting someone. You can say he is degrading women. I think the jury decided that those women went into the situation willingly and knowingly.

I don't want to drag you into the weeds of the Diddy trial. I just want to make the point that public sentiment is to not judge others. Not to use the force of the Federal Government to stop behavior we might not agree with. I think Diddy would have gone down hard if the prosecution had proven that he enslaved women and forced them to commit the sex acts they committed. But the prosecutors were unable to prove that, so they leaned on the idea that the public would want to punish him for his lifestyle. They were wrong.

All of this leads to law enforcement and prosecutors being hesitant to go after people for their religion or lifestyle. We have seen how fast public sentiment can turn against the government. So, it's a cultural problem. It's not the prosecutors' fault that they know the media is going to sway public opinion against them and that the public may be naive enough to go along with what information they are fed by the media.

And, it's the media's job to be skeptical of the government. The media is our shield against a government that would inevitably turn on its populace. As frustrated as I get when I see politically charged reporting that is pure propaganda to support an ideal the media wants to promote, the opposite of that would be worse.

To continue on with this thought at the risk of losing you, I will just say that the public maybe needs to be less lazy and pay more attention to what is going on. It takes effort to see through what is reported and get to the truth. We can't rely on one news outlet even if it supports our political views just because it reinforces our personal beliefs. We need to be willing to listen to the opposition. We need to be able to debate our friends and our family members without seeing them as our enemies. We need to not walk away when we are opposed. We need to think out our positions and be able to explain them to those who have an opposing position. We need to find common ground with people who disagree. I promise you we have more common ground than differences with those we disagree with.

So, is the only difference between the FLDS and terrorist organizations like Hamas or al-Qaeda that the FLDS resides in the U.S.? Of course not. The FLDS doesn't blow up buildings. They aren't militant in that way. They are equally as dangerous in my opinion, but sneakier about who they attack. And their attacks are not as noticeable as blowing up a building full of people. al-Qaeda wanted us to know who took down the Twin Towers. The FLDS would rather we not know of their crimes.

Still, they are doing all of the things noted at the beginning of this chapter. They need to be exposed. People need to know the truth. Real information should be investigated and reported on by the media. Maybe if the media gave political coverage a rest for a moment and reported on something else.

7

CHAD'S ALTERNATE REALITY

I said that our culture is at fault for creating a Chad and LVD and I believe that, but that is not to say that they have no fault. Of the two, which is the most at fault? LVD is probably the most hated between them, but only because she is the mother of Tylee and JJ. Chad didn't kill his own kids and I don't think he would have. But it was Chad with the ideas. It was Chad's plan that he and LVD were following. Chad is an evil monster. In spite of his boring, plain countenance, he is the evil force twisting minds to commit evil deeds on his behalf. He used this alternate reality to fulfill his desire for money, power and sex.

Idaho Prosecutor Rob Wood said:

"When he had a chance at what he considered his rightful destiny, he made sure no person and no law would stand in his way."

Chad was the one who laid out his alternate reality that LVD followed. She was already going down that path when she met Chad in 2018, but there is nothing that points to the idea that she was thinking about murdering her kids at that point. Not to say LVD didn't have a plan of her own. She surely did have a plan and Chad was a part of it.

Chad carefully laid out a detailed, apocalyptic belief system that allowed him to eliminate anything and anyone in his way. In the Chad Daybell trial in Idaho, Wood told the jury:

"...this was a convenient narrative; this narrative gave them the pretext to remove people from this world for their own good."

Saying "for their own good", he is talking about Tammy, Tylee and JJ. It was for their own good according to Chad and LVD, that they murdered them. This is what Chad had to convince people of in order for them to commit murder for him. First, he had to de-humanize his victims. They were dark. Their bodies had been taken over by zombies. They were really already dead. Then he had to convince Alex and LVD that they would be in a better place. This is where the idea of the Second Coming of Christ comes in.

According to Chad, the Second Coming was pre-ordained to occur on July 22, 2020 and it would be the end of the world as we know it. Few would survive. Many would die a horrible death, either by earthquake, floods or even worse; the plagues that would follow. Only the most worthy would survive and obviously Tammy, Tylee and JJ were not on that list.

The list of people who claimed to know the date of the Second Coming of Christ is long. The dates have come and gone as have the supposed prophets who prophesied the dates. Why some people still believe in anyone who claims to know when it will happen is hard to understand. I think there are many ingredients, but the first one is ignorance.

The very name of the Mormon Church says what they believe. The Church of Jesus Christ of Latter-day Saints refers to their belief that the return of Christ will happen sometime soon. Their whole religion is based on preparing oneself for it.

According to FAIR (Faithful Answers, Informed Response) a non-profit organization dedicated to providing well-documented answers to criticisms of the doctrine, practice and history of the Church of Jesus Christ of Latter-day Saints, Chad's end-times prophecy and the events he predicted prior to the Second Coming of Christ are not in line with Church teachings.

FAIR is not run directly by the Mormon Church, but it certainly exists to defend the Mormon Church. While it's not directly funded by the Mormon Church and it is a 501(c)(3) organization with non-profit status, most of its funding, if not all comes from donations from members of the Mormon Church, Deseret Books (a Mormon Bookstore), and conferences associated with the Mormon Church. Check it out and make up your own mind. Is it propaganda propagated by the Mormon Church or not?

So, are Chad's writings in line with Mormon beliefs or not? We could spend all day on this subject and not resolve it. We could talk to all kinds of experts and we would get differing opinions. I'll just say that I think most of what Chad wrote, especially in his books before he met LVD, are right in line with what the Mormon Church teaches. Not in a specific way, but in the sense that Chad believes the Second Coming of Christ will happen soon, good Mormons will be prepared for it, and it will be Mormons who are favored by Christ.

In fact, Chad's books were sold in the Deseret Bookstore and the Mormon Church had no problem with Chad or his books until he went too far. It's one thing to write about what life will be like for Mormons at the time of the Second Coming of Christ and it's quite another to say that one knows when it will happen. It's too bad people in the Mormon Church didn't see the danger when Chad started to believe or claim to believe that he could communicate with people on the other side of the veil, and they were telling him when the great Wasatch wake-up quake would happen.

Chad had always said his books were fiction. He wrote them in order to encourage thought. When Chad was starting to believe or claim to believe he could see through the veil and that he was an elevated being, he told his son, Garth that his books were true. In other words, according to Chad, they were scripture.

For sure, Chad and LVD's beliefs were on the fringes of the Mormon Church. Further, he professed to have answers the Mormon Church didn't have. He had knowledge beyond what the Church had. I wrote a lot about Chad's beliefs in my previous two books, but I'll add some information here.

According to Melanie Gibb, Chad had a theory about Zombies. People who were dark, could have their bodies taken over by an evil entity. That entity would work on the person's soul until there was nothing left of it. The soul would have left the body leaving only an empty shell inhabited by an evil energy. He used a light and dark scale to rate how far gone a person was. If it was early enough, and a person wasn't too far down on the dark scale, a person could be saved by prayer in what he called "castings". If it was too late, the only way to save a person was to kill the body. Their souls could then be released to Heaven.

We know that Chad and LVD love the book *Visions of Glory* by John Pontius and consider it scripture. Chad got his ideas from people like Pontius, Julie Row and others. Dangerous beliefs that fuel people like Chad Daybell, Warren Jeffs, Sam Bateman and many others.

Chad believed or claimed to believe that he was a translated being. He had lived multiple probations meaning that he had lived several lives on earth. He had even been married to LVD in past lives.

He believed or claimed to believe that he had had two near death experiences which opened up the veil allowing him to speak with people on the other side. People who had died.

But what does all this mean for all of us mere mortals? It means Chad is on a higher plane than we are. He is superior to us. God speaks through Chad and we had better obey him because the words coming out of his mouth are the words of God.

Unfortunately, and as hard as it is to imagine, a lot of people fall for this nonsense. But, even for those of us who know better, what are *we* falling for? We should all ask ourselves if we have beliefs that might be dangerous. Is it dangerous for us to believe we're Christians? Does that make us feel better than those who are not Christian? Think about it for a minute. Of course, a belief in someone or something that guides us in a Christian way is good. It is better than believing in something or someone that might be self-serving or hurtful to any other group of people or person.

Just like believing that being an American is better. Better because we believe in freedom, better because we believe in a government for the people, by the people. Of course, that does not mean that each individual one of us is better than anyone else no matter what country one comes from. It just means that as a whole we promote and defend the rights of each individual no matter what that individual believes.

But does our being Christian cause us to have beliefs that are dangerous? Does our being American cause us to have beliefs that are dangerous? It's easy to just say no, but in saying no, does that mean we think we are perfect? I don't think we're perfect. Far from it. So, what imperfections can we find in ourselves?

The imperfections of our country are easy to see. We have fought questionable wars. Our government feeds off itself growing and growing until the people feel helpless. Capitalism, which we must have if we are to be free in the first place, has allowed for a few people to be unbelievably rich and have too much power over the government and the people. So, it's imperfect and messy and we do need to constantly question it as we do.

But we are taught not to question our faith. It's in the very word "faith". We are supposed to have faith in a God we cannot see and that there is no evidence of. We hope that our prayers are heard. We never get an answer. In spite of some people claiming their prayers have been answered, if we look at it scientifically, the prayers that are "answered" can be explained by pure chance. They are anecdotal.

Even so, without our faith, without our belief in a higher being, a creator, what keeps us civilized? My answer to that is our faith in God keeps us civilized. Without our faith in God, it all falls apart. There has to be something more. There has to be a bigger reason for it all.

On the other hand, what if we lived our lives as though this one life is it? Wouldn't we be better off? What we accomplish here on earth, what good we do to make other people's time here better, less time spent worshipping a God we have to rely on faith to be sure of. Would that make us better? Would we focus on what's happening all around us and not on what we might find in the next life?

Don't look to me for the answers. I sure don't have them. The only thing I know is that I try to combine the two ideas and live my life the best way I can. I don't spend much time in church. I do worship God in my own way. I try to be a good Christian. I know I am very far from perfect or even as good as I would like to be. If I have to clarify, I would say that I feel like

I can be a better human if I spend my time being productive on Sundays or any day. I will still pray, but if someone is in need, I would rather try to find a productive way to help them and I think that honors God more than kneeling in church or listening to a sermon.

Don't misunderstand me. I have personally seen what I consider to be the hand of God work miracles through people. The miracle is performed by angels on earth. However, the angels don't descend from Heaven. They are human beings just like the rest of us. They have dedicated their lives to helping people in need. The true miracle is the combined knowledge they have, coupled with their willingness to sacrifice their time and effort to help others.

I'll dig my way out of this rabbit hole and move on by saying that I respect everyone's path they choose. Your path doesn't have to be my path. Your way of being a good Christian, a good human or a good American doesn't have to align with mine. Diversity is a good thing.

8

REXBURG IDAHO

I f ever there was a community that rode the fence between Mormon fundamentalism and the mainstream Mormon Church, I would say it's Rexburg, Idaho. In a lot of modern Mormon thinking it is an important place. On the same level as Zion (the site where God resides among his people). Some believe it is where the Second Coming of Christ is expected to occur. It will be the starting point for those Mormons who survive the imminent apocalypse on their way to Zion. It's where tent cities will be built in preparation for the journey.

A second temple is currently being built in Rexburg. There is the existing Rexburg Idaho Temple and the, under construction, Teton River Idaho Temple. Why does such a small town need two temples? Salt Lake City has only one Mormon Temple. A temple is not just a church. It is considered to be way more important. Not all members of the Mormon Church can enter a temple. One has to have a temple recommend from the Bishop. This new temple, the Teton River Idaho Temple is seen as a sign of the preparation for the Second Coming of Christ.

It's not just the mainstream Mormon Church predicting these events or saying Rexburg is where they will occur. It's the offshoot groups like AVOW (Another Voice of Warning) and PaP (Preparing a People). But, Mormons in the area are more isolated and in so being, more inclined to believe in these ideas. Not necessarily isolated geographically, but by the fact that 95% of the people living there are Mormon.

Rexburg was founded in 1883 by Mormons for Mormons. It was settled because people were attracted to the fertile ground for farming. It quickly became the second largest city in Idaho at the time. It is now home to Brigham Young University-Idaho where 99% of students are Mormon. There is a lack of outside ideas and influence. People are more susceptible to ideas like fundamentalism and the idea that the Church of Jesus Christ of Latter-day Saints is the one true church and all others are wrong. Not only wrong, but unworthy of Heaven. Not only unworthy of Heaven, but at the time of the second coming, at the mercy of Mormons. It will be Mormons who decide who lives and who dies, whose soul will make it to Heaven.

It is all of these things that make Rexburg a breeding ground for groups and individuals with fringe beliefs. It's what drew Chad Daybell from Springville, Utah to Rexburg, Idaho. Chad believed that in Rexburg he would be more able to thrive and grow. I think that people in Springville knew Chad's limitations and that's what held him down there. I think that Chad thought they just didn't see in him what his potential was. His bishop and others who knew him said he was kind, thoughtful and loved working with children. No one says they thought of him as any kind of leader. Just a good guy, good neighbor, good Mormon and a family man. Chad was stifled there, unable to move up the ladder. He was disappointed and began looking for answers elsewhere and outside of the mainstream Mormon Church.

In 2015 Chad's ward in Springville needed a new bishop. Chad had worked hard in his church and thought he should be considered for the advancement. He had even written several books which he thought would raise his standing within the church. His books are childish and single minded, mostly about life after and leading up to the Second Coming of Christ. But, in Chad's mind they were important books which gave a glimpse into the future. He was helping people prepare for the Second Coming which he thought (or claimed to think) was going to happen in the near future. He was not even considered for the bishopric though and that hurt him and made him feel overlooked. He began to look for other options. A way for him to advance and gain a larger following.

According to the prepper groups, the seven years of trials and tribulation that will occur at the Second Coming of Christ, will begin with the great Wasatch wake up quake which will be followed by floods, plagues and an even greater earthquake.

The Wasatch Front is the mountain range just east of Salt Lake City. It is home to one of the longest and most active earthquake faults in the world. Geologists believe a quake on the Wasatch Front is long overdue. There are many people exploiting this, claiming to have visions giving them insight into when the quake will happen. So, I guess Salt Lake and the people living there aren't expected to fare so well. Better to be in a place like Rexburg, Idaho. With all of the people claiming to have visions giving them dates for the earthquake, one of them is bound to get it right just by happenstance. I wonder if that person will be declared a prophet.

Rexburg, though, is closer to Yellowstone National Park. A supervolcano last erupted there 640,000 years ago and geologists say Yellowstone remains a living, breathing caldera. A magnitude 7.3 earthquake occurred in the area in 1959 killing 28 people and creating Quake Lake just outside of the town of West Yellowstone. Everyone in the western U.S. lives with the possibility of a big earthquake. There is a huge possibility of a supervolcano erupting in Yellowstone. We just don't know if it will happen tomorrow or 10,000 years from now. A relatively short time span in geologic terms. Geologists can't predict it any more accurately than that and neither can anyone claiming to have the voice of God in their heads.

I have spent a lot of time in Rexburg and I have gotten to know a lot of people from Rexburg. Like anywhere else, most of the people I have met there are clear thinking rational people so don't get the wrong impression. If you drove through there you would see a clean city with happy, friendly people. It's the kind of place where someone would still stop to help you if your car broke down. Just don't ask for a beer at a restaurant. You might get a blank expression from your server.

My first time in Rexburg occurred about thirty years ago. I took my family on an ill- advised winter drive from Northern California to Yellowstone. I remember we stopped in Rexburg for lunch. I was very impressed with how clean and organized the town was. Compared to what I was accustomed to, the town down right sparkled. At the time I had no idea about Mormonism and its influence on the community.

We rented snow machines in West Yellowstone and drove ourselves to Old Faithful. To this day, it is the most awe-inspiring vacation I have experienced. Now you have to go with a group and a guide. At the time I thought it was a little dangerous for my wife, myself and our two young children to wander through the park on our own in the middle of winter. We survived, but it was close a few times. The morning we left, it was foggy in the basin as it often is in the winter because of all the hot springs and thermal activity. As we drove through the fog on our snow machines we all of a sudden realized we were moving with a herd of buffalo. Very cool, but also very dangerous.

9

PREPPER GROUPS AND HUCKSTERS

In the trials of Chad Daybell and Lori Vallow Daybell, we learned about groups like Preparing a People and AVOW. I first heard of the book: *Visions of Glory* by John Pontius. I learned about podcasts put out by visionaries claiming to have a higher religious standing and answers that the mainstream church couldn't provide.

But what led to these groups? Why are we looking for answers? What drives people to think there are answers to questions there are no answers to?

Mormons and especially Mormons living in places like Rexburg, Idaho are living in a bubble. Outside ideas don't find their way into Rexburg very easily. If you've ever lived in a small town, you know that everyone knows your business. It's stifling. There is a hierarchy. There are the haves and the have nots. There are those who hold a lot of power and those who are subjected to that power.

Living in a place like Rexburg in the twenty-first century is in a way, like living in a religious protectorate in the Middle Ages. It's not that the church runs the government. However, the government is run by members of the church. Further, the church doesn't own everything like the FLDS did in Colorado City, but most things are owned by members of the church. Whether it's intentional or not, this creates a hierarchy. Powerful members of the church run things and have a lot of influence in the community. You must be in their favor and in their view if you want to better your standing within the community. So, in reality, it is the church that runs the community. Fortunately, we live in a democratic republic and not a religious protectorate so it only goes so far.

So, what are the problems with living in a community primarily run by members of the Mormon Church? What are the benefits? The benefits are easy to see. It's a clean, organized community with little crime and little poverty. The problems are more complicated and harder to see:

1. Ideas unapproved by the church are not welcome.
2. Influence comes mainly from the church.
3. People become afraid or skeptical of outside thought.
4. It's hard to overcome your station. In other words, if you are born into a family thought to be less favorable, it's hard for you to move up.
5. There is a hierarchy in the church which translates to a hierarchy in the community. People who hold high positions in the church hold high positions in the community and vice versa.
6. Living in an isolated monotone community leads people to want more. Human beings are naturally curious

and adventurous. It's in our nature to want things and to do things that may push boundaries.

7. A lack of outside thought and ideas leads to unanswered questions.

I think a lot of people find all of these things stifling. They begin to look for more. Because the church is so clear about ideas on marriage and sex and what is and what is not allowed if one wants to be a good Mormon, people go underground. They have to hide their involvement in what the rest of the country just sees as normal.

But, more than that, they start asking questions, seeking more information, looking for answers, questioning why they are different. Why is it so hard for me to be a good Mormon? Why do I want the things the church says are bad? If I'm gay, why can't I just be gay? If I like to look at pictures of naked people, why do I have to do it in the dark behind closed doors? Why do I have to stifle my normal curiosity about these things? This tends to make normal human beings, teenagers for instance, think something is wrong with them. They need to try harder, devote themselves more thoroughly and unquestioningly to the church.

I understand that the church would say we have to limit ourselves and not try to satisfy whatever selfish desires we have. There are obvious pitfalls to being free to do whatever we want.

But, not being able to at least talk about these things openly, not being able to express ourselves and ask questions, not being able to be different, being kept in the dark, only leads to the inevitable outcome of searching for more.

This opens the door to people claiming to have answers the church won't give. It also creates a community of people who are susceptible to those people. Also, a core tenet of the

Church of Jesus Christ of Latter-day Saints is to prepare for the disasters and difficulties that will occur before the Second Coming of Christ.

Chad caught on to all of this and used it to his advantage. Through author and speaker Julie Rowe, he learned that claiming to have a near death experience can be profitable and give a person a higher standing with a lot of people. He used the idea of near-death experiences to make the claim that he was able to see through the veil and actually talk to people on the other side; dead relatives, prior prophets like Joseph Smith and even Jesus himself.

Chad used this power he found over people to manipulate them. He convinced LVD to leave her husband, murder him and eventually murder her children. We can only understand how he was able to do that in the context of what I talk about in this book. Extremely naive, narrow-minded people are susceptible to believing that someone has the voice of God in his head. And, that you had better obey what this person is telling you whether it seems right or it seems like the most horrendous crime we can imagine.

Years of conditioning prior to LVD meeting Chad put her in a place psychologically to believe to this day that she and him are right in spite of all of the evidence that has been exposed against her. Her children are dead and she did that. How can the rest of us come to terms with that? Only by understanding how LVD's mind had been manipulated to a point where she is unable to understand what is real and what is snake oil.

She has to believe that her children, Tylee and JJ are in Heaven with their Uncle Alex doing good works. She has to believe that she put them in a better place and saved them from the coming apocalypse. She has to believe that the things she learned from Chad are right and the rest of us are just wrong.

10

LORI NORENE COX

I could have used several different last names for Lori, but Cox is the one she was born with. To this date she has been married five times. She married her first husband, Nelson Yanes in 1992 and divorced him in 1993. Her second marriage to William Lagioia lasted over two years from 1995 to 1998. She was married to Joseph Ryan, her daughter Tylee's biological father, for four years from 2001 to 2005. It took her only a few months after divorcing Joseph, to meet and marry Charles Vallow. Both Joseph Ryan and Charles Vallow are deceased. We know she is convicted of conspiring to murder Charles and Joseph's death is very suspicious even though it was declared to be from natural causes. She is still married to Chad Daybell and claims to still be in love with him.

But let's go back to her beginning. Lori was born in 1973 in Loma Linda, California to parents Barry and Janis Cox. The Cox's first child, Stacey Lynne was born in 1966 and died under unclear circumstances in 1998. We know Stacey Lynne struggled with mental issues and multiple disorders. She was Melani's mother. (More on Melani and her relationship with her mother in Chapter Twelve.) Her older brother Alex was born in 1968 and died under suspicious circumstances in 2019. Another older brother, Adam was born in 1969. I have gotten to know Adam. He was on his way to see Charles on the morning Charles was murdered. He had a somewhat distant relationship with Lori before she committed her crimes. Laura Lee "Lolly" was born in 1971 and died 6 weeks later in her crib. As mentioned above, Lori was born in 1973. Lori was followed by her sister Summer who was born in 1975. I have met Summer and have had only brief conversations with her.

Lori's parents, Barry and Janice of course are Mormon. Barry is an interesting character. He apparently doesn't believe that he or any of us for that matter should pay taxes to the Federal Government. In the late 1980s and into the '90s he refused to pay his taxes. In 2004 the U.S. Government sued Barry and Janice claiming they owed $300k in back taxes. The IRS won the lawsuit.

In 2018 the Arizona State Bar reprimanded Barry for falsely representing himself as a lawyer and he was barred from practicing law. In 2019, the year Lori's children went missing, Barry published an anti-IRS book called: *How the American Public Can Dismantle the IRS.*

It's really hard to get information about the family dynamic when Lori was a child, but we can see that it must have been abnormal. I have gotten to know and talk to a few close family members. Some say the family was in the realm of normal and another says it most definitely was not.

What we know is that the family had three children die of strange and questionable causes. First Laura Lee, then Stacey and then Alex. We know Alex was a serial murderer and Lori is a serial murderer. Alex was a convicted felon who lived mostly at his parent's home or with friends or relatives until he died at age 51. His first marriage lasted only a few months. His ex-wife claimed that the family dynamic was strange and that Lori and Alex had a weird sexual dynamic that freaked her out. Alex later married Zulema Pastenes at Chad's insistence and took her last name. Zulema's description of her time with Alex is extremely strange. I describe it in my first book.

So, even with a lack of concrete evidence that there was an at least unsettling family dynamic, I think it's fair to make the assumption. Lori had an overbearing zealous father, a weak beaten down mother, death was part of her early life and there was an at least weird sexual dynamic. We can't say for sure that Lori had been sexually abused by her father, but I will say I think it's a possibility.

I can tell you that the number of women who I have met since I started writing my books who were raised in abusive Mormon families would shock you. Of course, a father sexually abusing his children is a problem in any religion or outside of religion, but I will say that it seems to be a particular problem in heavily patriarchal religions.

Prior to marrying Charles, Lori's previous marriages were full of discord, drugs and even violence. I don't know if it's true or not, but Lori has claimed that Joseph Ryan abused her son Colby and daughter Tylee. Two of her prior husbands are deceased and one is on death row in Idaho waiting for his date with the firing squad.

When I think about it, if she had come clean when her kids went missing and admitted to her part in things, I could almost feel sorry for her. Don't worry, I do not. And, she has not once asked for any forgiveness or admitted to anything. Instead, she has put everyone through three trials, insisting she is innocent in spite of all of the evidence against her and in spite of multiple convictions and her five consecutive life sentences in Idaho and her two consecutive life sentences in Arizona.

The question I have kept asking myself almost from the beginning of my involvement is: How did we produce a Lori Vallow Daybell? My premise is that we are responsible for her. Don't take that the wrong way. I don't mean to say that anyone is directly responsible for her actions but her. She committed the crimes she committed. None of us were even aware they were happening.

But, how does one get to a point where she can do the horrible things she did and feel justified? Even more than that, feel like her crimes were actually acts of love.

Let me break it down in two parts. Part one being what influence the people around her had on her, and part two being how she feels okay with what she did.

I describe what I think her early family life was like above. She was born into a family that was dealing with the death of a baby. This might cause one to be somewhat impervious to death. Were Lori's parents still mourning the death of Lolly when Lori was born? Her family system was extremely patriarchal. Being a girl, she would be made to feel less than. I think that would have been hard for her to accept and she would rebel. It would also affect her relationships with men. There was at the least a very strange sex dynamic within the family.

Her family was very Mormon and appearances were important. Even if there were problems within the family, those problems would have to be hidden from those outside of the family. Image and appearance are important in Mormon culture. Always put up a good front. Some of her relationships with men were violent.

So, in light of all of that, how does she feel okay about her brutal murders of purely innocent people?

I think she developed an over heightened sense of self. She became selfish. It was all about her. Her world became small, focused only on what she could obtain for herself. She became unable to feel normal emotions like sympathy or love. She learned that by manipulating people, she could get the things she wanted. She became very good at it. She became open to ideas like those that Chad was espousing. This is what finally led her down the path to murder. She was overwhelmingly selfish, extremely manipulative and open to ideas that she was above everyone else. Smarter, prettier and more elevated. She came to believe that she has a special relationship with Jesus. Seems like a common thread.

To this day, LVD claims to still be in love with Chad, even though in Chad's trial, Chad and his attorney John Prior claimed she was the one behind all of the murders. She claims to believe that the Second Coming of Christ is imminent, but it will be on Christ's time, so hard to predict exactly when it will happen. She claims to have conversations with Chad's deceased wife, Tammy and that they are good friends. She also claims to have conversations with Tylee and Tylee forgives her and tells her she did nothing wrong.

She says that all of the deaths were of natural causes or were accidents. I know that was how it was supposed to look, but it's astounding that she is sticking with that claim. I think it did work for her in the cases of brother Alex and husband Joseph, but she has been convicted of conspiracy to commit murder in both Idaho and Arizona. At some point one would think she would just give it up. No one believes her and she has nothing really to gain by lying at this point. Just shows her lack of a sense of what is real and what is in her head.

She seems to believe she is actually a qualified attorney even though her own trial was a disaster. She is supposedly giving legal advice to her fellow inmates. She says God put her where she is to help those inmates. She makes herself sound like a hero who we have all victimized through our ignorance of the court system and how corrupt it is. I take issue with that.

One of the problems that I feel rising in myself is that Lori is becoming familiar to me in a way that creeps me out. I have been a juror sitting daily in trial closely watching her reaction to the evidence the prosecution was presenting. I have attended in person and watched her Arizona trials on Court TV. I have watched all of her interviews, some more than once. I have watched all the videos I can find on her. I have had eye contact with her a few times.

One time in AZ as we all came into court and I found my place in the gallery, she turned from her table and looked at me for a long time. As uncomfortable as that was for me, it was another of those times when I was determined not to break eye contact. That would make her think I am afraid of her. She began with a puzzled look. Then a look of recognition. Then a look of forgiveness.

It's her way of trying to manipulate me without saying a word. Bring me into her fold. And she gives me a look like she knows me, a kind of knowing smile as if to say, "I know you and what you are doing and I forgive you." Obviously, I can't know what is going on in her head, but that's the feeling I get and I don't like it. Anyway, I feel like I have had so much exposure to her, I have spent so much time studying her, that she has become familiar. The word "familiar" has the same root as the word "family" and she feels that familiar to me.

I have made a deal with myself that she is coming back to Idaho shortly after her sentencing in Arizona and she will be out of my life forever. When I am done with this book, I will be done with her to whatever extent that is possible while I continue to investigate and write about the FLDS, PaP, AVOW and whatever the current cultish abuse system is.

11

CHARLES VALLOW COMES INTO THE PICTURE

Of course, Charles Vallow didn't come onto my radar until my experience as a juror in the Lori Vallow Daybell trial in Idaho in 2023. This was four years after he was murdered in Arizona. I have, however, become good friends with his sister, Kay Woodcock, and his brother, Gerry Vallow. They are good people and have nothing but good to say about their brother Charles. Gerry's stories about growing up with Charles in Lake Charles, Louisiana are priceless. A look into a past that I'm afraid we're losing in this country.

Charles and Gerry grew up a lot like I grew up in approximately the same era, playing ball, chasing girls, cruising main and generally being boys.

Charles and Lori met and were soon married in 2006. Even though Charles had divorced his wife, he was a pretty well squared away guy. He had played college baseball and had even been looked at by scouts of Major League Baseball. He was a "southpaw" (left-handed) pitcher and, according to his brother Gerry, he was a good one. If he hadn't blown out his shoulder Gerry believes he would have pitched in the majors.

According to friends, Charles was a happy guy, easy to be around and hard to rile. As an adult, he loved living in Texas, the Austin night life, and was a fan of University of Texas football. He had a good career and made good money.

When Charles met Lori, he had two sons living with his ex-wife. Even so, Charles had a close relationship with them and they loved their father. Charles was a financial advisor and his career caused him to travel around the country, so it would have been hard for him to raise his boys on his own or even to split custody.

Charles loved Lori's kids and had no problem being a father to them. In fact, Lori's son, Colby says Charles was the only real father he ever had. Charles was always there to support Colby and Tylee.

When Charles' sister, Kay Woodcock, approached him in 2014 with the idea that he and Lori should adopt JJ, he didn't hesitate even though raising JJ would be a challenge. At the time Lori was considered by people around her to be a good Mormon mom and she accepted JJ with open arms.

Kay and her husband, Larry had taken JJ home from the hospital after he spent several weeks there having been born premature. Kay and Larry loved JJ and only a grandparent understands the challenge of raising children in your 60s. And, JJ did have autism and was all over the place, but Kay and Larry loved that about him.

Like so many of our young people nowadays, JJ's biological parents struggled mightily with drug addiction and were unable to care for JJ. I wrote more about that in my previous two books. I have since had the opportunity to meet JJs biological father. He is working hard to turn his life around and I believe he has a good chance. I truly hope he makes it. He is in a better position than most of us to use his voice to help others.

Charles and Lori had a happy marriage for 11 or 12 years. Charles even joined the Mormon Church to support Lori and promote a good Christian lifestyle for his adopted children.

Around 2018 Lori began to spend more time at church. She bullied the bishop of her church to give her a "Temple Recommend" so she could spend time there. She went to the Temple almost every day.

Not all Mormons have access to the Temple. One has to have a high standing in the Mormon Church to have that privilege. One has to be current on his or her tithing and no black marks on their record. One must adhere to the standards of the Church demonstrating chastity, honesty and faith. Not how I would describe LVD.

As time went on, Lori became more and more obsessed with her religion. She told Charles that she spoke personally with Jesus and he answered her. Charles began to worry, but tended to laugh it off and do his best to support her until he realized something more was wrong.

It finally got to a point where Charles realized it was some kind of mental illness. Most of us have had relationships with people who are a little less than stable. There is never a simple answer or solution to anything. Everything is hard and everything is your fault. When it's someone you truly love, it's extremely hurtful. Everything you do to try to help blows up in your face. Still, you keep trying.

This is the point where Charles involved the police in Chandler, AZ and this is the point where I can only conclude that the police let Charles down. None of the murders that came after had to happen. I have seen firsthand that LVD is a master manipulator, but the signs were there for anyone to see.

I wrote about the night Charles came home from a business trip in Chapter 10 of *Chad Daybell, The One Mighty and Strong.* What he told police was terrifying and it should have been obvious that the lives of not only Charles, but of Tylee and JJ, were in danger. Lori had exhibited behavior that showed she was dangerous and Charles gave evidence to the police and literally begged them for help. He wanted not only protection for him and his family, but also help for Lori. She was able to manipulate the people in the institutions that exist to deal with these situations. It was just too easy for her.

Charles had also reached out to Lori's family for help. He got no help from any of them except her brother Adam. Adam was doing what he could to help Charles until Charles was murdered by Alex and Lori. Adam even traveled to Arizona from Texas and had a meeting scheduled with Charles to see what could be done. That meeting was supposed to take place right after Charles took JJ to school. When Charles didn't show up, Adam just assumed he had been blown off by Charles and had no idea until later that day that Alex and Lori had murdered Charles.

This certainly should have convinced the police that Charles had been right and Lori was dangerous. But no, they accepted Alex and Lori's stories of self-defense in spite of all the evidence that pointed to murder, and set them free. Free to murder again, and again, and again.

With Charles out of the way, Lori could continue her courtship with Chad. Her only obstacles left were Chad's wife, Tammy and her own children. Tammy and the children would have to go also.

12

MELANI BOUDREAUX

(NOW MELANI PAWLOWSKI)

It's very possible that Melani Boudreaux was taken under her Aunt Lori's spell and the wider spell of religious zealotry. Lori's sister Stacey, who was Melani's mom, died when Melani was only nine years old. Of course, the family stepped in and did their best to fill the void for Melani. Filling the void though, also meant filling her head with dangerous ideas.

So, the question is: Do we give Melani a pass? Is she a victim or might she be guilty of conspiring to have Alex murder her estranged husband Brandon Boudreaux? Do we believe she has awakened from the spell she had been put under in her developing years? I think the truth is the truth, her crimes are her crimes and our laws are our laws. If she did conspire in the attempted murder of Brandon, we need to expose that and charge her with her crime.

This is one of the most frustrating issues for me. When I ask prosecutors in Idaho if she might be charged with crimes, they refuse to give me any kind of answer. I was confused by that until I found out there is an open investigation into her in Arizona. I didn't know that until I sat through LVD's trial in Arizona and Prosecutor Treena Kay said it in court. Now that makes sense. If she committed crimes, those crimes were committed mostly in Arizona. The only crime I can think of that she may be guilty of in Idaho would be covering for Chad, LVD and Alex's murders of Tammy, Tylee and JJ. Not to diminish how big a crime that would be and I hope the prosecutors in Idaho are looking into it.

I haven't been able to find out much about the investigation in Arizona, but I'm assuming they are trying to gather evidence that proves she conspired with her Uncle Alex and Aunt Lori to murder her then husband, Brandon Boudreaux. Sitting through LVD's trial in Arizona, it felt like Melani was more on trial than LVD. Her name was brought up by the prosecution constantly. Was Treena Kay giving us a glimpse into the future? Kay is a bulldog of a prosecutor, but to be honest, I don't trust the state of Arizona. Arizona has let us down over and over again in this case. I just have to hope that Kay has the freedom to pursue Boudreaux (now Pawlowski).

Brandon is the only one of Chad and LVD's targets who we know survived. We know from LVD's trial in Arizona that she conspired with her brother, Alex to murder Brandon. Why would she do that? Why would she care if Brandon lived or died? One possible answer is that LVD was doing a "good deed" for her niece. Getting Brandon out of the way would give Melani freedom to pursue her religion. It would give Melani financial security from Brandon's life insurance policy and the total of the proceeds from the house they were selling that they owned together as husband and wife. Just like Charles,

Brandon is a successful businessman. LVD and Melani may have thought it would be profitable to murder Brandon.

Melani was in the process of divorcing Brandon, so it would also obviously give her full custody of her and Brandon's children.

It's a weak argument though. LVD was selfish and I doubt she would murder Brandon just to help out her niece. There had to be more to it. Melani was in Chad and LVD's inner circle. LVD and Melani went to the Temple together almost every day which is excessive. It was causing problems in Melani's marriage because it was keeping her from her responsibilities as a mother and a wife. Melani was becoming unduly influenced by Chad and LVD, believing in their ideas about religion and believing that Chad had higher powers. Chad's influence over Melani was becoming weird. We know she called him "daddy". It gives me the creeps.

Melani is a looking glass into the dangers of religious zealotry and those who preach those ideas. She is an interesting individual and I think gives us more of an insight into the influence a religion can have on a person. Studying Melani and her past has given me a better understanding of what drives a person to a place where their perception of reality becomes flawed. How someone's upbringing and the religious influences in their lives can lead them to a place where they feel they are being crushed by the very people and things that are good in their lives.

Melani's then husband Brandon, her supporter and the father of her children was eventually seen by Melani to be a roadblock to her future and her goals. Brandon was as innocent as Tammy Daybell or Charles Vallow. He was and is a good father, he was a good husband and a good Mormon. He was a good provider. He was and is everything a husband and father should be. His only goals in life were to protect and provide for his family and be a good role model for his children. He cherished his family and loved them all with his whole heart. He would do anything to keep his family intact. I have met Brandon and his family. I watched him testify In LVD's trials in Arizona. He strikes me as a sincere, caring human being and everything I describe above.

I'm going to take this opportunity to make my position on the Mormon Church and the members of the Mormon Church clear. I have met and gotten to know many members of the Mormon Church who are truly good people in every possible way. They embrace what is good about the Mormon Church. There is a lot of good. The values of family, parenthood, work ethic, providing, giving and more are good values. I have a lot of respect for members who promote these values and I hope they know that my criticism of their church is not a criticism of them or of those values.

Melani's mom, LVD's older sister, Stacey died when Melani was nine years old. She had been struggling with an eating disorder and very likely other psychological disorders. She wouldn't let Melani attend school or even play with other children. She was worried about what germs Melani might be exposed to. She controlled Melani's diet to an extreme. She would follow Melani around with disinfectant. Stacey's husband, Melani's father, did his best to reason with Stacey, but the situation became hopeless as Stacey's condition, whatever it was, worsened.

Melani, like her Aunt Lori, strived to be a good Mormon. Consider the world view of a young girl becoming a young woman growing up isolated and conditioned the way Melani was. No school, almost all food is bad, germs are everywhere, everything will make you sick or hurt you, and then finally your mom, your protector dies of something she taught you to be afraid of. Then consider the influence someone like Aunt Lori would have on her. Lori became Melani's mother figure.

Let's look at the situation at the time of the attempt on Brandon's life and we can make up our own minds about Melani and her possible involvement.

Brandon and Melani are going through a contentious divorce. They are selling their house planning to split the proceeds. They are battling over custody of their children. Brandon has a restraining order on Melani which Melani breaks over and over. The police are involved enough to know the situation.

I describe Alex's failed attempt to murder Brandon in *"Chad Daybell, The One Mighty and Strong"* so I won't go through that here. I will just add to it what I learned in LVD's conspiracy to commit murder trial for her involvement in it.

Alex missed hitting Brandon in the head with a high-powered rifle by about an inch. The only thing that saved Brandon was the trim above the window on the driver's side of his Tesla. One inch lower and the bullet would have gone through the window and hit Brandon's head. Even a half inch lower would probably have done the job. If the bullet would have bounced off the trim it still surely would have hit Brandon in the head. As it was, the bullet went into the trim and I guess disintegrated. Knowing high powered rifles and the damage they do, I am amazed that Brandon was so lucky.

And the gun Alex was using was a semi-automatic rifle. If Brandon had hesitated even for an instant, Alex could easily have gotten off at least one more shot. Having been shot at point blank myself, I know that your brain takes over and you react quickly without thinking. There is no time to be afraid until you think back on it. Thinking back on it, you can't explain why you did the things you did. I'm sure Brandon hit the accelerator and sped off before he even knew what he was doing or what had just happened to him.

When I mention to people that I have been shot at point blank, they always want me to tell that story. I will do it here as an aside. If you aren't interested in my personal experience, just skip the next six paragraphs.

I have actually been shot at twice. Once while riding my motorcycle in an area known for illicit marijuana growing. I had a helmet on and I kept hearing a strange zinging noise. After the third one I realized it was bullets whistling past my head. I got out of there in a hurry!

The other time was a lot different even though it happened within a mile of the first time. The little Northern California community I lived in had been primarily a logging community. As environmental strains reduced the cutting down of trees and good paying jobs, people were turning to cultivating marijuana. However you feel about cutting down trees and growing pot, it destroyed that community and a lot of others in the area.

Anyway, my small declining town was holding one of its last logging shows. If you have never experienced a logging show, let me tell you, it was very entertaining and also very dangerous. More so, I would say than the annual rodeo held in the same arena. Ax throwing, relatively safe unless someone gets mad, tree climbing, log rolling, chain saw competitions.

Pretty rough in the stands too looking back on it. Loggers and the like were tough individuals prone to fighting.

As I sat in the top row of bleachers with my sister, niece and nephew, I happened to look down and behind the stands where a fight was taking place. No big deal. I noticed a few of my friends watching the fight and as it concluded I made my way down to catch up with them. Just as I was approaching my friends, I noticed a guy walking toward me in a long duster type coat like the ones you might have seen in a western movie. Not too out of the ordinary in that time and place, but just as I noticed him, he pulled out a gun. He was within just a foot or two of me then and before I knew what was happening, my arm shot up knocking his hand up as the gun went off. I had reacted without even knowing it. The bullet must have missed my head by inches at the most. I had never seen this man before and he could have had no reason to single me out.

You would think that firing a gun with intent to kill in a crowded area would land a person in jail. He was not prosecuted, but I heard he did die in a logging accident a few years later.

Anyway, I feel like this experience gives me a little insight into how Brandon reacted when he was shot at by Alex. Watching the police video of Brandon right after the shooting, I can see what I believe to be Brandon coming to terms with what had just happened to him. His mind was calming down and he was able to think clearly. It took him a while to realize what should have been obvious to him. Alex just tried to murder him. He must also have been asking himself why and realizing that his own wife just tried to have him killed. That would be not only terrifying, but also very sad for him. His whole world must have changed in that moment.

We know that Melani was in contact with Chad and LVD when Alex made his attempt on Brandon's life. We know she had a motive. In fact, I would say she had more of a motive than LVD and LVD has been convicted of conspiring to murder Brandon. I guess the question is, do they have enough evidence? I guess we'll see.

What about Melani's affiliation with Chad and LVD in Idaho at the time of Tylee, Tammy and JJ's murders? She was practically living with LVD having moved to Rexburg with her and having an apartment in the same complex. Chad told Melani to get away from Rexburg to avoid the police.

I can see no possible way that Melani didn't at least know that Tylee and JJ were dead before their remains were found in Chad's backyard. Melani's father, who had been divorced from her late mom Stacey, sent Melani a letter begging her to tell what she knew. He later told LVD's brother Adam that his daughter, Melani is as guilty as Chad and Lori. So, in Idaho, I think she is at least guilty of protecting Chad and LVD.

I've always wondered about Melani's current husband, Ian Pawlowski and his relationship with Melani. It seems to me that any sane man would have run for his life when he found out what Melani was involved in with her Aunt Lori, Chad and Uncle Alex. They didn't get married until November, 2019. That was after everyone was murdered. He could have gotten away unscathed.

Prior to Tylee and JJ's remains being found in Chad's backyard on June 9, 2020, it seems like Ian was cooperating with the police and FBI who were investigating their disappearance. Ian had only known Melani for a few years at this point and he was doing his best to support her. He wasn't trying to cover for her or hide anything. He believed that Melani found herself in an impossible situation and he wanted to help her wind her way through it. He felt like Melani had been led down a dangerous path by Chad and LVD.

At some point, Ian lost faith in the police and FBI. He felt like they were going after Melani without reason, treating her unfairly. It seems to me that Ian was thinking clearly in the beginning even if he was blinded by his love for Melani. He never fell for Chad and LVD's manipulations directly, but I feel like it all eventually seeped into his mind. Even if he didn't believe all of their ideas about religion or their beliefs, he was still influenced by them in some way. They were able to convince him that the police were being unfair to Melani. He doesn't seem to take into consideration the gravity of missing Tylee and JJ and how determined the police and FBI were to find them.

In Ian's affidavit and interviews with law enforcement, we can see that he was very involved in the investigation into the missing children. He even recorded phone calls with Chad and LVD behind Melani's back. He was trying to protect Melani from the police, Chad, LVD and Alex.

I cannot tell from everything I have read, if he is genuine in his belief that Melani was duped by Chad and LVD or if he is covering for her involvement. And, if he is covering for her involvement, is he doing it because he believes she was duped, or is it because he knows she's guilty? This is one of the as yet unanswered questions that haunts me. Neither he nor Melani will answer my queries. I'm sure their lawyers have told them not to talk to anyone, but it does seem like an opportunity to explain themselves and I sure wish they would.

13

WHO IS ALEX COX?

One of the keys to understanding LVD is understanding her brother Alex. How did Alex come to be a cold-blooded killer? We know it wasn't his idea to murder anyone. He did it for his sister. Did he enjoy it? Did he get some kind of psychopathic, sadistic thrill out of murdering innocent people? Or did he simply do it because he thought Chad and LVD lived on a higher plane and knew better than he did what was best?

I think it is an unfortunate combination of the two. I think he did get a sadistic thrill out of killing. I also think he thought Chad and LVD somehow had a higher spiritual standing and in fact were in communication with Jesus. Chad had convinced him that the second coming was at hand and that evil forces were working through his victims. Convincing Alex that Charles, Tylee, JJ, Brandon and Tammy had been invaded by zombies and were really just shells of human beings, their souls already having departed, dehumanized them and gave Alex an excuse to fulfill his desire to kill.

But, what kind of mind is susceptible to believing such things? That's what we need to understand. To understand that we need to know about Alex's childhood, his family life, his religious background and whatever other influences that may have made him who he became. Let's start with his own death and work backward from there.

Alex died of a double pulmonary embolism in his lungs. What that means simply is that both of his lungs were compromised by something and it killed him. What his lungs were compromised by could have been many things. Some kind of untreated disease, drugs, poison, a heart condition. Because the timing of his death was so suspicious, law enforcement and the medical examiner looked into it thoroughly. If Alex took or was given drugs or poison that caused his death, those drugs or poison must have been very hard to detect. Unfortunately, Alex's body was cremated as soon as it was allowed. Cremation is not common among Mormons and we know Alex wanted to be a Mormon even though he had been excommunicated from the Church more than once. He always strived to earn favor back in order to be brought back into the fold.

The only thing we know for sure about Alex's death is that it was extremely convenient for Chad and LVD. It happened just a few days after Tammy's body was exhumed and the autopsy was performed, which indicated that the police were aware that her death was suspicious. It also came the same day Chad gave him a blessing saying he would be a translated being. Before all of the trials, the only people we are sure who knew that Tammy's death was murder were Chad, LVD and Alex. Alex was a bit of a goofball and Chad and LVD didn't trust him to keep his mouth shut. I think he would have sung like a canary.

Alex came off to the people around him as just kind of a sad clown. A simple guy. He was a jokester who loved to laugh and tell jokes. But, there had to be so much more to Alex. In the videos I've watched of him, I see a man who looks harmless. He looks like he would be a fun uncle.

He never had much going for him in life. He was an underachiever in his family for sure. He drove trucks off and on, worked as a comedian and appears to have done just enough to get by. He seems to have been dependent on his family to get by though. When LVD moved to Rexburg to be with Chad, Alex went along and rented an apartment in the same complex.

We get a glimpse into who Alex really was from Zulema Pastenes' testimony in court. In *"Money, Power and Sex"* I write about what she had to say. She was certainly not comfortable in her marriage and I think only married Alex because Chad told her to. I think she was looking for a way out of the marriage when Alex died. He died in her bathroom. That raises questions in my mind about Zulema. Could she have had a part in his demise? I really don't know. I will say that I have pondered the idea that Alex did not die of natural causes. I think LVD and Chad were most likely behind his death. I just don't know if Zulema may have had a part in it or at least have known it was happening.

Another thing we know about Alex is that an ex-family member says Tylee was afraid of him. Tylee's friend said the same thing. Why would Tylee be afraid of Uncle Alex? Did Tylee know he murdered Charles? She was supposedly outside of the house with JJ when Alex shot Charles, but I have some doubts about that. Did she see Alex shoot Charles in cold blood? Or, did she get the creeper vibe from Uncle Alex? I think that's very possible. Alex was known to frequent prostitutes, he had a freaky encounter with Zulema that made her question her marriage to him, he had a strange sexual relationship with his sister Lori, and his ex-wife left him because she realized he was weird. Tylee was just coming of age and I think Uncle Alex made her uncomfortable at the least.

Of course, now knowing that he murdered her, dismembered her body and burned it, I think it's more than safe to say Tylee had reason to be afraid of him. I also think that the sharp point injuries to her pelvic bone, which were pointed out by the medical examiner in his testimony in Chad's trial, indicate that Alex had a sick perversion directed either at his niece or women in general.

When Alex and Lori's sister Stacey was sick, and on her deathbed, Alex was left home alone with her while the family was in Hawaii. Alex called the family and told them that Stacey was under hospice care and was dying. The family didn't come home from Hawaii until Stacey was dead. That is suspicious to me. Was Alex left home to murder Stacey? She had serious psychological problems and was causing problems for the family. Could it be that Alex was a murderer before Chad came along? On behalf of his family? I don't think we'll ever know the answer to these questions.

PART II

THE TRIALS OF LORI VALLOW DAYBELL

14

THE STATE OF ARIZONA VS. LORI VALLOW DAYBELL

(CONSPIRACY TO COMMIT FIRST DEGREE MURDER OF CHARLES VALLOW)

My wife says I like to rant. She's not wrong. I rant about politics, I rant at stop lights, I rant about whatever game I'm watching. It's the injustice of it all. Or I could say it's the human condition. The way we are forced to live. Whatever it is, I can't seem to not do it.

You may have detected a rant or two in my writing. I try hard not to do it. It's not fair of me to subject you to it and I very much doubt you are interested in my rants. Still, sometimes I can't help myself.

I found myself ranting more than usual when we were in Phoenix for the trial. I realize that I'm not terribly fond of Phoenix. If you live there, don't take it personally. It's just not what I'm used to. It has its own kind of beauty and culture. So, try to forgive me if you catch me ranting in my description of the trial and my experience there.

We rented a really nice apartment right across from Chase Field, home of the Arizona Diamondbacks Major League Baseball team. I am a San Francisco Giants fan, but unfortunately the Giants wouldn't be playing the Diamondbacks while we were there. Still, I am a baseball fan, so we did go watch the Diamondbacks beat up on the Milwaukee Brewers.

It was about a mile walk from our apartment to the courthouse. Downtown Phoenix is laid out in a grid, so we had a choice of which roads we walked on. Even in early April in the early morning, it was hot. We quickly realized that we would pick our route based on which felt the safest. None of the ways we could go felt very safe though.

There was one small tree on the route we had chosen and there was a homeless guy apparently living under it on the sidewalk. We just walked on the other side of the street to avoid him. Thinking back, I wonder if it might have been better of us to have walked by him and at least said good morning. Maybe hand him a bottle of water. My experience with homeless people is what made me want to avoid him, but couldn't I have given him the benefit of the doubt? I was on a mission to get to the courthouse and hopefully at the head of the line.

Like Ted Bundy, Charles Manson, Warren Jeffs and Lynette Fromme before her, Lori Vallow Daybell would waive her right to an attorney and represent herself in her trial for conspiracy to commit murder of her late husband, Charles Vallow.

There is something in the psyche of a cold-blooded murderer that makes them so narcissistic that they think they can represent themselves in court better than a highly trained lawyer. Wherever LVD's narcissism came from, it would certainly take center stage in this trial. It was immediately apparent to me that LVD believed she could manipulate things in court; the judge, the jury and possibly even the prosecution. She certainly thought she could manipulate the witnesses she or the prosecution would call to the stand.

I would not miss the opportunity to see it in person. Not only would it give me the opportunity to gain insight into Lori Vallow Daybell (something I have been pursuing for two years), it would also give me the opportunity to spend time with the family members and others who I had become close to since LVD's trial in Idaho ended. An added benefit turned out to be that I would meet some new people who were able to provide me with even more insight.

I guess I have to admit that as immersed as I am in this case, as invested as I am in the truth behind her crimes and as much as I want to represent the victims, there is an element of entertainment value in watching LVD represent herself. She is hurtful and abusive to her living victims. She is disrespectful of the justice system and the court. She scoffs at anyone who opposes her or calls her on her lies and her crimes. It's a good thing the judge demands silence in the gallery. If allowed, there would have been cheers when witnesses or Judge Beresky put her in her place. If we accept the idea that there is entertainment value, the best of it was when she was exposed for who she really is, when her transparent attempts at manipulation backfired.

I was impressed with how composed some of the witnesses were in their testimony. People who she hurt. People she tried to murder. Some whose lives will never be the same. LVD was frustrated that she couldn't rattle them. I was taken aback by her obvious desire to hurt them even more. She was given the opportunity to address them in court. To ask them questions that they had no choice but to answer.

Watching all of that unfold taught me something about her. Her ability and desire to cause pain is unending. She is a person who will murder innocent, weaker people, people dependent on her, even her own children, in the most brutal and painful way. What I really learned is that she didn't just murder Tylee and JJ because they were in her way. She didn't do it to, as she says, send them to a better place. She didn't just have someone else murder for her because she wouldn't be able to do it herself. She did it with malice, hatred and a desire to cause pain.

All of that puts her right where she belongs. In prison with no chance of ever being free. No amount of self-inspection and remorse will ever change that. Not that she would ever question herself or feel any remorse. But even if she did, there is no mechanism for her to find her way out of where she put herself. No time off for good behavior, no parole. Just one life sentence followed by another and another on and on.

The only question that remains for me is what life is like for her in prison. According to her, she is working with her fellow inmates, helping them fight the "unjust" justice system. Using her vast knowledge of the legal system. She has fallen so far that the only people who might fall for her nonsense, the only people she can be exposed to, are people who have been deemed too dangerous to live amongst the rest of us and have no choice but to cohabitate with her.

Just like the Chad Daybell trial in Idaho, I had to get to the courthouse early and get in line in order to make sure I would get a seat in the courtroom. A line would form outside the courthouse and as soon as the doors were opened, it was a race through security and up to the fourth-floor courtroom. Judge Beresky was able to secure a bigger courtroom than had been originally planned in anticipation of a large crowd, but it was still very small, and on some days, not everyone was able to get in.

Just like in Idaho, people traveled from around the world to see this trial. A couple from Australia who I had met in line at the Chad Daybell trial in Idaho showed up in Arizona for this trial. A lot of the faces were the same. Trial watchers, true crime enthusiasts and media were all in line every morning waiting for the show to begin.

Fortunately, I was able to get in everyday, despite some people cutting the line. I have to thank podcaster Joe Schmoe for keeping track of when everyone showed up, and my wife for having the guts to point out to the bailiffs those who were trying to jump the line. It was always the usual suspects. 99% of the people in line were respectful and able to monitor themselves. But, like in any group of people there are disruptors. People who could care less about fairness and seem to have no limit to their selfishness, causing drama and discord wherever they go. Unfortunately, these people aren't satisfied with simply being rude and inconsiderate. They are still doing their best to cause problems among some of us who strive to live purposeful lives.

We are all aware that we are exposing ourselves to these kinds of people. We do it willingly for the greater good. We are motivated by making a living for ourselves by doing something positive and important. We do our best to ignore those who would try to tear us down and just go about doing what is right.

Just like in the Chad Daybell trial, waiting in line was far from a waste of time. I met Mike Watkiss for the first time. I had no idea who Mike was, but I could tell he was somebody. Mike turned out to be a wealth of information for me. I thought it was like fate that we met since we both understand how deep the problem of religious fundamentalism is and that the problem is far from solved when LVD is convicted.

I had never met or had a conversation with Treena Kay. After the trial was over, I sent her an email with a list of questions. She was kind enough to respond, but unwilling to talk about the trial. When I first watched her in court, I wasn't sure what to make of her. She came off to me as stark and harsh. I thought she was the opposite of prosecutor Lindsey Blake in Idaho. I guess stark and harsh are qualities you would want in a prosecutor. I found out over the course of the trial that she is also very thorough and precise. I did meet her and got the opportunity to chat with her after the sentencing. I found her to be warm and interested when talking to her in person. Of course, I had to find a way to weave Melani Boudreaux (Pawlowski) into the conversation, but she was unwilling to comment on that. I take that as a good sign that Kay might be planning to charge her.

After experiencing two trials with Judge Boyce in Idaho, I guess I thought he was exceptional and I wasn't expecting Judge Beresky in Arizona to live up to the same level of competence and dignity. I was wrong. Judge Boyce and Judge Beresky are both exceptional and Judge Beresky had a seemingly impossible job, keeping LVD in line in court. LVD was hostile toward him, but he was somehow able to keep his composure and remain dignified. I could tell that LVD couldn't comprehend why she was unable to manipulate him. In her mind, she thinks she is in control of everything and everyone. It shows how narcissistic she is. In spite of the fact that no one is falling for her lies and manipulation, she keeps doing it expecting a different result.

Judge Beresky kept everyone in line and heading in the right direction. I could tell it was a challenge for him at times. I think he even stopped LVD from telling the jury she was a translated person. She was heading down that road at one point when he stopped her and suggested a break. When we came back from the break, LVD took a different tack. I really wanted to see the looks on the jurors' faces when she told them she had walked with Jesus and had a personal relationship with him. I was disappointed when Judge Beresky stopped her even though I understood he did it to avoid the possibility of a mistrial.

Judges are different from most of us. I watched Judge Beresky and Judge Boyce in court. I've had conversations with Judge Boyce outside of court. I have a judge in my family. None of them seem to want any kind of recognition. They don't seem to want attention. They truly do their best to remain neutral. They are not the story. I believe they would say that if they do their job correctly, we wouldn't remember anything about them. We do though. I wonder if they get the appreciation and acknowledgement they deserve. I hope so.

There were very strict rules about what the jury could know about LVD. I thought it was unfair to the jury and unfair in terms of the trial that they could not know that she had been convicted in Idaho. I could understand if she had simply been accused and not yet convicted of her horrible crimes there, but the truth is she is a convicted murderer in Idaho currently serving five life sentences. That seemed like pertinent information to me.

If a convicted serial arsonist was sitting in court accused of starting a fire, I would think the jury would know. His past would indicate a proven tendency for starting fires. A criminal's rap sheet shows a pattern.

Also, what if the jury, not knowing she was a convicted murderer, was not able to convict her? What if they found her innocent or acquitted her and found out immediately following the trial that she had murdered her children? How would that have made them feel? Fortunately, they got it right.

I wonder if there was a bit of a juggling act by the prosecution and the judge. Could they have weighed the options and decided it was best to leave some things out of what the jury was told in order to make a cleaner trial? Could they have left some things out in order to protect the police and hide their mistakes? They will never say.

The media was outside the courthouse ready to pounce on the jurors as soon as the trial was over and the verdict had been announced. They seemed a little confused by the questions they were getting. I had been wondering if any of them might have known more about LVD than they admitted, but I could tell by their reaction to the questions they were getting that they had no idea.

I was not impressed with how the jury was managed in Arizona. I thought a lot was left to chance and that was dangerous. People had a lot invested in this trial. It was an important trial for many reasons. Important for the victims' families to see justice, important for the community the crime was committed in to see justice and important for law enforcement and prosecutors. Allowing the jurors to inhabit the same areas as the public during breaks seemed like it could turn into a disaster. Trusting the media to leave them alone ended up working out, but why risk it?

Picking a jury so fast left a lot to chance. Potential jurors were not given time to understand the importance of the trial. The judge and attorneys didn't take the time to weed out those who might not be up to it. Would they be able to get to court every day? Would they be able to be on time? Would they be able to focus on the testimony and give the trial its due? Would their own lives be too negatively affected by what they were about to be involved in? In the end, it worked out okay, but there were certainly some hiccups and things could have gone very wrong.

Day One 3-31-25,
Maricopa County Superior Court, Phoenix, AZ

The back row of the gallery was reserved for the media and the front two rows for the family of the victim. The middle three or four rows for the rest of us. It was a scramble as people had an idea of where they wanted to sit. Some wanted to be in a position they thought would give them the best view of LVD. Some who had followed people like Lauren Matthias wanted to be close to her. I preferred to be where I could see the jurors, but really, I was just happy to be in the courtroom and couldn't care less where I sat or who I sat next to. The bailiff who was in charge of the gallery had an idea of how he wanted people to enter the courtroom and be seated. I think he was a little surprised and put off by some people trying to sideswipe his directions.

At this point I am sitting in the courtroom listening to Juror questionnaires. Detective Nathan Duncan is sitting at the prosecutor's table. He is the case agent and was one of the primary investigators in the investigation into the murder of Charles Vallow. He's a big guy, so easy to spot. I remember him from his time on the witness stand in both trials in Idaho.

LVD is immediately hostile with Judge Beresky, trying to manipulate him. She has a few attorneys to assist her at her table. LVD is running her part of the show though. I think the main purpose of her attorneys is to keep her on track. And let's be honest. The whole trial was set up in a way that would hopefully be successful. Neither of LVD's attorneys spoke in court. They were court appointed I think just to make sure she couldn't later say she was under represented. The only thing I ever saw them do was whisper in LVD's ear. I'm sure they had a lot to say to her outside of the courtroom. They must have explained it to her when she was opening doors for questioning that would hurt her case.

Here's what I mean by that: LVD had proven herself to be a pain in everyone's ass. She was likely to be disruptive and disrespectful. She had proven that in pre-trial hearings. Not only would the judge have to keep a tight rein on her, but also, the prosecution would have to do her job for her. LVD had no idea what she was doing. The prosecution didn't want a mistrial. If LVD blew up, the trial would be in jeopardy. It would have been easy for prosecutor Treena Kay to go in a direction that could cause those things to happen. Instead, if she wanted a clean trial, Kay, having a good understanding about how trials should go, would have to guide things in a positive direction. I'm sure Kay had evidence that she would like to have brought in that she didn't bring in thinking it would cause LVD to go off the rails. As entertaining as that would have been, it would not have been in the best interest of a fair, clean trial.

LVD was also wearing a racc (remotely activated custody control) belt. Judge Beresky had a choice of having her wear cuffs on her wrists and ankles or having her wear a racc belt. He went with the racc belt because it could be hidden under her shirt and wouldn't clue the jury into the fact that she was a convict already. LVD argued that the Marshal said she could go unrestrained in court. I don't know if she misunderstood the Marshal's recommendation or if she was outright lying, but Judge Beresky read out loud what the Marshal actually said. She needed to be restrained and a racc belt was an option.

A marshal sat just a few feet from LVD and I assume he had the button that would activate the racc belt. Unfortunately, we never got to find out. It would have been fun. When activated a racc belt delivers 50,000 volts for 8 seconds. It is able to subdue a very large angry man, putting him on the ground with severe pain and muscle spasms. It can also lead to loss of control over bodily functions. I'm sure the psychological effect it would have over a smallish woman would be enough to make her think twice before crossing whatever line she would have to cross to cause its activation. I'm also sure it was made clear where that line was drawn. She could have gone with the option of ankle and wrist restraints. That would not only have been obvious to the jury, it would have restricted her movements.

In Idaho jurors are paid $10 per day for the first five days and $50 per day from then on if the trial goes longer. In Arizona jurors are paid up to $300 per day unless their employer pays them for their jury service. They also are paid mileage to and from court. They did have to pay for their own lunch and I was surprised to find them in the courthouse cafeteria with the rest of us. Even though in Idaho we weren't sequestered, we were very much isolated from the media. A juror would have had to go out of their way and somehow avoid the guards who were always there in order to talk to anyone in the media.

Arizona averages about 30,000 violent crimes per year compared to 4,600 in Idaho. Arizona has 7.91 violent crimes committed for every 1,000 residents. Idaho has 2.31 violent crimes for every 1,000 residents. So, maybe Arizona has a harder time finding enough jurors unless they pay them.

Day Two 4-1-25,
The Jury

Judge Beresky began day two by saying he thought they would have a jury by the end of the day. This surprised me since it took two weeks in the trial I served on in Idaho. It also concerned me. I understand how much of a hardship it is for people to serve in a trial of this magnitude. Not only is it hard for people to be away from their families and work, they are exposed to things that are emotionally taxing. My concern was that jurors weren't given enough time to fully understand what they were getting into.

In Idaho we were questioned over and over again about whether or not we would be okay with seeing the things we were going to see. We were also questioned over and over again about what we may have known about the case. Judge Boyce, his assistant and attorneys on both sides had plenty of opportunity to see if someone was being dishonest or just not understanding what they were getting into.

Sure enough, right as the trial was set to begin, two jurors claimed hardship. They could have done that before the jury was finally selected, but I just don't think it was given time to sink in for them. It's kind of like buying a new car. In the showroom everything is exciting and new. If you give yourself the opportunity to sleep on it you have time to consider the whole picture. The payment, the practicality and all of the negatives. Given enough time to contemplate how it is going to affect your life, being a juror is a big commitment. Yes, it's our duty as citizens, however as citizens if it is a hardship, we are given the opportunity to say no. It's important to take the time and fully consider whether or not as a juror a person will be in a frame of mind to give the trial it's due.

And on opening day, we had to wait for three jurors to show up. On most days, the court had to wait for jurors who were late. If getting to court on time was going to be a hardship for those jurors, they should have said so. If a person can't be on time, I have to wonder if they are serious enough people to be good jurors.

In the end, we did have a jury by the end of day two. 13 men and 3 women. 4 of the 16 would be alternates and it worked the same way it did in Idaho. The alternates wouldn't know who they were until the trial was over and the jury was about to deliberate. I described my feelings about finding out I was an alternate after sitting through five grueling weeks of testimony in *Money, Power and Sex.*

I was surprised by the fact that men made up such a high majority. I remembered in Idaho, the last thing Judge Boyce did before certifying the jury, was that he looked over the jury and declared that no particular type of person was over represented. I can't say for sure, but I believe that if there had been such a high majority of men, he would have declared that the jury was over represented by men.

I heard some people in the gallery mention that they thought the majority of men would work in LVD's favor. Having been a man on a jury that convicted her, I disagreed. I have seen that her wily ways have worked on men in the past, and I do believe that she may have thought it was to her advantage to have a lot of men on the jury, but her crimes are too serious and she has lost whatever power she may have held over men in the past. Maybe I am biased knowing so much about her, but there is absolutely nothing appealing about her looks or her mannerisms. I suppose Chad Daybell is proof that there are men in the world who are stupid enough to fall for her nonsense, but I think they are a rare breed.

Other than more men than women, the jury looked like a pretty good cross-section to me. There were older people, younger people, light skinned people and darker skinned people. If looks are an indication, there were members of the LGBTQ community as well as people who appeared not to be. Just like in Idaho, there were note takers and non-note takers.

It felt strange to me and somehow not right for LVD to be able to question potential jurors. Of course, it was her right since she was representing herself, but knowing of her crimes and convictions in Idaho and watching her have conversations with people who had no idea what she was convicted of seemed wrong.

LVD was obviously nervous when she stood up and approached the jury box for her first opportunity to talk to the potential jurors and ask questions. She hesitated so long that it became uncomfortable. Several times she looked at her notes and then to the jury and I wondered if she might lose her composure before the trial even started. I've seen actual attorneys hesitate for a purpose. It can build anticipation and make the question seem important. Maybe that's what she was doing, but it sure didn't feel that way to me. It felt awkward.

When she finally pulled herself together and began to speak it was in her little girl voice. I've heard her use that voice before, but it's not her normal voice. She saves it for situations where she wants to come off as innocent and helpless. Other times I have heard her voice be domineering and demanding. I wonder if she does it subconsciously or on purpose.

Her first question for the jurors was whether they could find her innocent even if she didn't testify or take the stand as a witness. Then, would you have difficulty understanding a family dynamic? (I have a lot of difficulty understanding hers). Then, could you stand alone if you disagreed with the majority? Obviously, she is hoping to win at least one juror over. It's her only hope.

Then she made a bizarre statement which the prosecution objected to. She said the jury was here to protect her from the state. Judge Beresky clarified for the jury that they are not there to protect her from the state, but to decide if she is guilty or innocent based on what they see and hear in court.

Her voice was so quiet and child-like that it was hard for me to hear her. She was repeating herself and I thought she was losing the jury already. She is trying to sound submissive and at the mercy of the jury. She is certainly at the mercy of the jury, but I don't think she is in any way submissive. It's just a tool in her very limited tool box. It's like using a sponge to drive a nail. Not very effective.

One huge difference in the way trials are run in Arizona as opposed to Idaho is that in Arizona, jurors are given the opportunity in open court, to ask witnesses questions. I would have loved to have been able to do that. I was surprised that in this trial, it only happened a few times though. I'm afraid I would have had a lot of questions. Some of the questions I thought the jury might ask as this trial progressed may have caused problems for the judge and the prosecution. I wondered if any of the jurors might have had any knowledge about LVD's crimes in Idaho. Even if they didn't, I thought they would ask why Tylee or JJ weren't called in to testify. As far as the jury knew, they were the only ones still alive besides LVD who were at the crime scene. Tylee would have been 22 years old and certainly able to testify.

I guess Judge Beresky had some control over what questions could be asked. The questions would be written down and handed to him by a bailiff. He would read it to himself and then out loud to the witness. It didn't come up, but if he felt like the question was inappropriate, he could have told the jury that he wasn't going to read it.

Day Three 4-7-25,
Opening Statements

LVD started the day by objecting to Brandon Boudreaux being in the courtroom. Judge Beresky called for a sidebar. I would love to have been able to hear that conversation. The Judge and LVD were going at it pretty hard. When it was over Beresky said Boudreaux could stay. He had been on LVD's witness list, but she dropped him before the trial started. LVD having him on her witness list would have been a smoke screen anyway. She never intended to have the man she tried and failed to have murdered testify on her behalf.

As a witness for the prosecution, he would not have been allowed to sit in the courtroom, but as a victim he had a right to be there. One of those weird twists not covered by any clear law that would have to be decided by the judge. I'm guessing that in the sidebar Kay said she would not call Boudreaux to the stand unless LVD did something unexpected causing her to need to. So, if LVD didn't bring him up, the prosecution wouldn't bring him up. His day was coming in the next trial.

I know that Boudreaux did have some information that would have been pertinent to this trial. He knew Charles well and they even did some business together. He could have testified about Charles' fear of LVD and the fact that Charles was trying to get the family to help him. He could have stated that he thought Alex had tried to murder him also. I'm sure that would have been objected to, but he could have said it. I just think Kay knew she didn't need Boudreaux's testimony to get a conviction.

In Idaho when a sidebar was called, the attorneys would get up and approach the bench. The judge would step down to the side of his bench, white noise would be played just to make sure the jury or gallery didn't overhear what they were saying. It was all very time consuming. So, I thought the fact that they stayed where they were and used headphones in AZ would be better. The only problem was that the headphones failed to work more times than not. When they didn't work, we would have to wait for the technicians to come in and fix the problem. I noticed that after the second or third time the technicians stayed in the courtroom.

All I could see was the back of her head as Treena Kay stood up to give her opening statement. I have never seen hair as straight and neatly trimmed as Kay's. Half way down her back and obviously very recently trimmed to perfection. I try not to make judgements on people's appearances, but in this case, it seemed obvious that Kay was making an effort to come off as trim and straight-forward. It put me in mind of FBI Agent Doug Hart who took a big role in convicting LVD in Idaho. All business. It was a stark contrast to LVD's Shih-tzu hair.

I will note here that no charges were filed in Arizona against LVD or Alex until June 24, 2021, two months after she was charged in Idaho.

In her opening statement, Treena Kay gave a brief run-down on the events of the day Charles was murdered by Alex almost six years before this trial. I will repeat some of it here to give you a better understanding of the testimony that was given in court:

In 2019 Lori and her husband Charles Vallow were separated. Charles had rented a house in Chandler, Arizona for Lori, Tylee and JJ to live in while he lived in the house they had all previously lived in. Charles would not have had to rent a house for her. He did it to try to keep the family as happy and safe as he could.

I describe the separation in my previous books, so I'll just say here that it was contentious. Charles had loved Lori and did everything he could to get through to her and keep his family together. Lori was diving deeper and deeper into her zealotrous religious beliefs. She seemed to be always either at the temple or dancing in front of her mirror covered walls. When Charles was unable to get through to her, he did every-thing possible to get her help. He pleaded with family members and friends of Lori, but got no help.

When he returned home from a business trip in January of 2019, he found his truck missing from its parking space at the airport. When he finally got home, the locks on his house had been changed. Charles called the police. I have seen the body cam video of his conversation with the police in two trials and watched it several times on my own.

Charles is seen pleading with police hoping he can get some kind of help with Lori. He tells police that he is afraid for his life and the lives of Tylee and JJ. He says they had a great marriage for 13 years, but that Lori has had some kind of mental break. She believes she knows when the Second Coming of Christ will happen.

"She says I'm Nick Schneider" he said. "I have taken over Charles' body and Charles was killed."

Police agreed to have Lori committed and evaluated at Community Bridges, a mental health clinic in the area. Charles met the officers outside the hotel where Lori had been staying, but she was not there.

Lori went to the police station to file a report that Charles had stolen her purse. She alleged that Charles had been cheating on her while on his business trips and that she had kicked him out of the house. She was very good at manipulating the truth and telling outright lies.

Lori was with Melani Boudreaux and when she found out that the police were looking for her to commit her, she decided she would voluntarily check herself into Community Bridges. While there she told the people that she and Charles were simply having marital problems and that Charles was as much a part of those problems as she was. She apparently convinced them as she was released just a few hours after she checked in.

A few days later, Charles filed for divorce and a protection order for him and JJ against Lori. Lori retained custody of JJ even though she didn't seem to want to be responsible for him.

Charles and JJ were very close and Charles hadn't seen JJ in a long time. He and Lori agreed that Charles would come to the house on the morning of July 11, 2019 to pick JJ up and take him to school. For Charles, it was just an opportunity to spend some time with JJ. I don't believe that Charles had any clue that it was a trap set in order to murder him.

Charles had tried to get help from Lori's family. He had hoped that her parents would try to reason with her, but no one except Lori's brother, Adam believed Charles. Charles asked Adam to travel from Texas to Arizona to meet with him so they could work out what Charles could do to help Lori. They were to meet after Charles picked up JJ and dropped him off at school. Charles never made that meeting and Adam was left wondering why. He soon found out that Alex had shot Charles and killed him and was claiming self-defense. Adam wasn't buying it.

Why murder Charles? Lori thought she was the beneficiary of his life insurance policy. She had been until Charles changed it to his sister, Kay. Charles felt like Kay and Larry Woodcock would be the best people to take care of JJ if something happened to him. Kay and Larry loved JJ and had proven themselves. Killing Charles was a win-win for Lori. She not only thought she would receive the money from his life insurance, but she needed him out of the way so she could marry Chad Daybell.

Remember, this is a conspiracy trial. Did LVD conspire with her brother Alex to murder her husband, Charles? In her opening statement, Treena Kay laid out the evidence she had against LVD. She claimed to have texts between LVD's brother Adam and Charles. Those texts would show that Charles was nervous about LVD because she had said threatening things to him. After Charles entered LVD's house, LVD took his phone and wouldn't return it when he asked her to. Kay posited that she did that to keep Charles from just leaving what turned out to be a threatening situation, giving Alex the opportunity to shoot him. LVD left with his phone and wallet after Alex shot Charles.

After Alex shot Charles and LVD left, she called Alex twice before he called 911 forty-seven minutes after he shot Charles. When police arrived and Alex exited the house, he had sunglasses on his forehead. How could that be if he just had a fight with Charles?

"Physical evidence does not lie."

LVD followed Treena Kay with her own opening statement. In contrast to Kay's perfectly manicured hair, LVD's was more "poodle" like, or "Shih tzu" maybe. Not to make fun of her, but that's the only way I can describe it to put the proper picture in your head. She was allowed to wear civilian clothes rather than her prison uniform. She dressed professionally in Hillary Clinton style pantsuits. Even knowing it was there, I wasn't able to notice the racc belt.

She said her and Charles had been married for 13 years and it had been a happy marriage. They had moved from Austin, TX to Chandler, AZ in 2009. She claimed that Charles had been a Triple A baseball pitcher. He was a southpaw (left-handed) pitcher, but batted right-handed. (I went to a Diamondbacks game with Charles' brother, Gerry on one of the evenings after trial and asked him about that. He said Charles absolutely batted left-handed. He would know having grown up with Charles and spending his childhood playing baseball with Charles.)

LVD went on to say that Tylee was three when she and Charles married. Her previous husband, Joseph Ryan had died of a heart attack and Tylee had been receiving Social Security benefits for about three years since his death.

LVD began to appear to tear up when telling the jury that her and Charles had a lot of arguments during their marriage. She claimed that Charles had taken JJ out of school. (As we know from her trial in Idaho, it was her that disenrolled JJ from school). She told the superintendent that JJ would be home schooled. At this point, I was wondering if the jurors could see through her obviously contrived tears. I hoped so. I knew they wouldn't have any way of knowing that she was telling them what I and others in the gallery knew to be lies. It would be Treena Kay's job to expose them.

Describing the events on the day Charles was murdered by Alex, she claimed that Charles was aggressive toward Alex and they ended up having a physical altercation. When that started, Tylee ran outside and Charles came after LVD with a bat. LVD ran outside and Alex shot Charles shortly after. JJ had been struggling to get out of the car seat he was strapped into in Charles' car. Tylee was doing her best to keep him strapped in. (At this point LVD pauses to get a Kleenex). So, Shih tzu hair, wearing a racc belt and 5 life sentences for conspiracy to murder in Idaho and I'm not buying her tears. She knows very well though that it's not me she needs to convince. It's just one juror of the 15 remaining jurors.

She drove off with Tylee and JJ to take JJ to school. The gates weren't open yet so she took Tylee to get flip flops. We were later shown a video in court of LVD purchasing flip flops at a Walgreens in Chandler. She paid cash for the flip flops. When her and Tylee returned, they were interviewed by police who forced them to stay across the street from the house away from Alex.

When asked if she would come to the police station to give a statement, LVD volunteered to do so. She and Tylee were driven to the station in a van and Alex was driven separately from them in a police car. The police asked LVD to turn over Charles' phone which she did, but Tylee was reluctant to give them the passcode. This was true, but was Tylee just being an obstinate teenager, or was she trying to hide something for her mom?

Police gathered Charles' belongings from his hotel room. Five months later Alex died of natural causes. LVD finished by saying that:

"Family tragedy is not a crime."

I heard her say that before at her sentencing in Idaho. Throughout her statement she kept saying:

"The evidence will show."

She never did produce one piece of evidence that showed anything.

The State's first witness was officer Owen Wersbecky who was first on the scene the day Alex shot Charles. He said Alex was nonchalant and compliant. After placing Alex on the curb, Wersbecky entered the house, cleared it and found Charles' body. He went into the bedroom where Alex told him he had placed the pistol he used to shoot Charles and retrieved it. EMT's had been waiting down the street for the scene to be cleared and it was safe for them to come in. They follow a strict protocol not to arrive on a scene that hasn't been secured by the police. They stage up somewhere close to be as ready as possible as soon as the scene is secured.

In her cross-examination of Wersbecky, LVD had a few moments of victory. Or, at least I thought so. She asked that if Alex had performed CPR on Charles, wouldn't that have pumped out what blood Charles had left? Her point was that it would have been better for Alex to wait for EMT's to perform CPR. It did not, however, explain why it took Alex 47 minutes to make the call. She also asked why he thought it was strange that Alex was acting nonchalant. Wersbecky denied saying the word nonchalant. He clearly did say it and I was getting nervous already about the police in Arizona, and if they were going to get through this trial without revealing how incompetent I already thought they were. Sorry to say the TV show Reno 911 came to my mind.

I'm going to take a moment here and clarify my position. I have nothing but respect for our police officers. They have an impossibly hard job. They put themselves between us and dangerous individuals who would do us harm. They perform heroic acts like running into buildings with an active shooter. My family has personally experienced them going out of their way to help us through hard times. They are held to a higher standard as they should be and they seldom let us down. On the whole, they are the best of us.

However, my impression of the Chandler Police Department in this case is that the standards are low and that points to a systematic failure. I can give them the benefit of the doubt while pointing out what I see as weaknesses or failures. We need to be able to do that. We need to be able to be critical. We need to be able to praise those who do the job well and criticize those who do not. We need to be able to question them when we see what we think is a failure. That is our duty as citizens.

After a brief re-direct by Treena Kay, I was shocked when Judge Beresky asked the jury if they had any questions for the witness. They did not, but like I said earlier, I didn't experience that in Idaho. I would have loved the opportunity to ask questions of witnesses and I would surely have done so. It gave me a little thrill though thinking of the future possibilities. What questions might they ask?

Next to take the stand for the State was Chandler P.D. Officer Robert Krauthiem. He had 25 years of experience and said that Alex's demeanor was different from what he would have expected from a person who had just killed someone. No sweat, no jitters, no trouble speaking. He was calm and nonchalant as was Lori when she showed up. That word "nonchalant" kept coming up. I think he brought it up on purpose to "clean up" after Wersbecky. It was pretty transparent and I was again thinking of Reno 911.

Krauthiem then said that Detective Nathan Moffett showed up and took over the interview with Alex.

In her cross-examination LVD asked questions that had nothing to do with anything. She would do that a lot. She did her best to look the part of an attorney, but she failed miserably at it in my opinion. A lot of questions about how many miles it was from the police station to her house and how long it would take to make the drive. I'm sure people who didn't know her were waiting for her to get to the point. I wasn't. I knew from past experience there was no point.

At this point I assumed the next witness would be Detective Nathan Moffett. As Krauthiem mentioned in his testimony Moffett showed up and interviewed Alex while he was sitting on the curb. Moffett had been the case agent during the investigation. His testimony in the Idaho trials was significant and important and I was looking forward to what he would have to say in this trial.

In Idaho he stated that he did not think the wound on Alex's head was consistent with being hit by a baseball bat. That would certainly be important for this jury to hear. In Idaho he also said that the bullet on the floor under Charles' body indicated that Charles was laying on the floor at the time of the second shot. Moffett also interviewed Alex further at the police station. Moffett never did testify in this trial.

Next up was Chandler Firefighter Scott Cowden. We were ripping through the witnesses. Cowden testified that if Alex had performed CPR on Charles, it would have left an impression on Charles' skin. He testified about the condition he found Charles in. He had to wait in his firetruck 30 seconds away from the house until it was cleared and safe for him to approach. As soon as he got the call, he drove up to the house.

When he entered his first impression of Charles was that he was not breathing and that there were no signs of life. He said he noticed there was no impression in Charles' chest like he would expect if someone had performed CPR at the 911 operators' instruction. As Cowden immediately began CPR on Charles, he felt and heard the "crack" he expected.

When performing CPR and pushing down on the chest, the ribs crack in the sternum. I didn't know that and apparently neither did Alex. Anyway, the EKG Charles had been hooked up to was just showing a flat line indicating it was unfortunately over for Charles. Cowden then inspected Charles' body. He found 2 exit wounds. When he said this my thought was that if 2 bullets exited Charles' body, there should have been blood splatter. No one testified that there was any blood splatter and the pictures I saw in court of Charles laying on the floor showed no blood splatter.

Cowden went on to testify that Charles' skin was pallid and there was significant lividity. Lividity occurs after the heart quits pumping and blood is forced down to the lowest part of the body by gravity. It looks like bruising.

Cowden was very clear that he didn't think Alex had performed CPR. That is significant for two reasons. It would show that Alex was lying to police and it would show that Alex just let Charles lay there and die.

Day Four 4-8-25,
Things Don't Add Up

More problems with the jury. Juror #4 was released. Juror #16 wanted out also, but Judge Beresky refused to release him. This is what I was afraid of. We're just beginning and we've already lost one juror and another's heart isn't in it.

They clearly should have been more selective. People serving on a jury in a murder trial are subjected to pictures and other subject matter that is not for the weak of heart. They don't understand the effect it is going to have on them until it's happening. They see it on TV all the time, but this is real. The tears of the family members in the gallery are real, the victim is real and the enormity of it is just now becoming real to the jurors.

In LVD's cross-examination of Cowden, she tried to get him to say that it would be hard for a first timer to perform CPR.

In Kay's redirect she got Cowden to explain that 911 operators are trained to help people perform CPR.

I would like to pause here and try to give you a feeling for what it was like for me sitting in an Arizona courtroom watching LVD try to defend herself. I have to say (if you haven't noticed) that I have mixed feelings about the court system and law enforcement in Arizona.

I think I started out not expecting a very high standard of professionalism and a will to give the job its due. I think that came from all the videos I watched and the facts of the case. I do think more could have been done for Charles earlier.

I will say though, that as the trial progressed, I became more and more impressed with Prosecutor Kay and with Judge Beresky. Phoenix is the 5th largest city in the U.S. Downtown is rougher than what I am used to in Boise. I have been all over San Francisco, LA and other cities and it seems like the bigger they are, the dirtier they are and the more crime there is.

Maricopa County Courthouse is huge, encompassing two 16 story towers, so it naturally feels less personal than the Ada County Courthouse in Boise. To be fair, I spent a lot less time in the Maricopa County Courthouse than I did in the Ada County Courthouse, so I didn't have as much time to get to know the folks who work there.

All this to say I went in with low expectations. I was more impressed than I expected in some ways and in other ways it was about what I expected.

The courtroom was somewhat smaller than the Courtroom #400 in the Ada County Courthouse. There was a big area just outside the door with chairs for people to sit on while they waited to be let in. That was nice and I spent a lot of time gleaning information from some of the people there and talking to people who had read my books.

Even in early April it was hot in Phoenix. Some days it was over 100 degrees. In a city made of nothing but concrete, let me tell you, that's hot. In the courtroom though, the air conditioner was blasting away. I learned after suffering the "arctic blizzard" for the first few days to bring a sweater.

The courtroom itself was what you would expect. Very similar to other courtrooms I've seen. The gallery faces the judge, the jurors to the right, the prosecution on the right in front of the gallery and the defense on the left in front of the gallery. The first two rows of the gallery were sectioned off for the families of the victim and of LVD. There were a lot of family members of the victim and once again, not one person was there to support LVD.

I can't figure out why we still do this, but there is a court recorder repeating everything that is said into a microphone. Seems outdated to me.

Chandler Fire Department Captain Kent Keller described the scene of the shooting of Charles. Charles was found lying flat on his back with his head facing north. The bat was lying on the floor to his right and his baseball cap was on the floor above him (north of him). His hands were laying to his sides and there was a noticeable gunshot wound to his chest. A bullet was found on the floor under his body and there was very little blood on the floor. The walls in the living room were covered with low mirrors, but there was no furniture.

My thought at that point was that LVD had time to place mirrors on the walls, but no time I guess to put any furniture in the house to make JJ and Tylee comfortable. In the pictures I had seen, there were no beds in the bedrooms and no table in the kitchen.

Charles had mottling-patchy skin caused by a lack of oxygen. His pupils were dilated and non-reactive. There was lividity caused by a lack of blood flow which indicated that Charles' body had been there for a while. There was no active bleeding and no heartbeat. Keller didn't observe any injury to Alex. He did overhear LVD talk about a pool party they were planning for that afternoon.

Before bringing in the next witness, the judge, prosecution and LVD had a debate about his expertise. The question was: How is bullet trajectory relative to conspiracy? LVD wasn't being accused of firing the gun. Everyone agreed that it was Alex who shot Charles.

I thought LVD brought up a good question and I wondered if it came from her or her attorneys who were only there to assist her. Kay's answer to it was even better though:

"First you have to prove it was murder."

Chandler P.D. Detective Daniel Coons had 30 years under his belt and was a sniper instructor and a crime scene reconstruction expert.

I have to say that this is where things get a little weird for me. The jury is instructed to convict or acquit based on the evidence. If they question the evidence presented, I would think that would cause doubt. And remember, they have no idea that she has been convicted in Idaho. They know nothing about her except what they are seeing in court. What they are seeing in court is just a woman representing herself, claiming to be innocent.

I'm no detective, but things didn't seem to add up to me. There were many things about it that didn't feel right and I was left with unanswered questions. We were shown videos and sketches and I just couldn't see how it could have happened the way they were saying. I'm sure at this point, that if I were on that jury, I would be asking questions in open court about how the police conducted their investigation. They would have had to show me more for me to accept their story. Things just weren't adding up. Their story was too pat and there were a lot of things I thought were left out.

The most obvious thing in the prosecution's favor, and the thing that everyone understood, was that the second bullet Alex fired into Charles was lying on the floor under Charles' body and there was a fresh divot in the floor very apparently caused by the bullet. That didn't fit with what Alex told police and it indicated that Charles could no longer have been a threat to Alex. In cases of self-defense, one is supposed to quit shooting when the threat has been neutralized. That is very clear and the first thing one learns in a conceal/carry class.

But there were other, less obvious discrepancies. I couldn't see any blood splatter or any blood under or around Charles' body. Charles had been a minor league baseball player. He had, according to Alex, taken a bat from Tylee and attacked Alex with it. Alex had a small cut on his head he claimed was caused by Charles hitting him with the bat. The bat, however, was lying on the floor several feet from Charles' body which was laying on its back. It was also to the left of Charles' body (on Charles' right side).

Okay, that's a little vague and the bat could have gotten where it was in several ways. It may have been inadvertently kicked out of the way by first responders. It may have ended up where it was while Alex and Charles struggled. However, there were other factors that made me suspicious.

Alex was facing Charles when he shot. Just to his right there was a rounded or curved wall. Alex was standing next to the curved wall in the opening of a hall that opened into the living room. Two casings were found together to Alex's left against a straight wall. My thought was that the shell casings would have ejected out of the pistol to Alex's right, so why did they end up to his left? Kay addressed that and Detective Coons explained that when the casings were ejected from the semi-automatic pistol Alex was shooting, they bounced off the rounded wall and ended up just inches from each other against the wall to the left.

I thought it would be unlikely for the casings to bounce off a rounded wall and end up that close together. Especially since the angle of the pistol would have to have changed when Charles fell to the floor. Alex's first shot would have been somewhat parallel to the floor. His second shot would have been at a sharp downward angle. This would have drastically changed the path of the casings as they ejected from the pistol. And, Charles was lying in the middle of the living room when Alex took the second shot. Alex would have to have moved away from the hall and into the middle of the living room. He would have to have been standing over Charles. The casing would have to have been to Alex's right in the living room probably against the baseboard several feet to Alex's right.

I wondered why there was no blood splatter from Alex's first shot. He shot Charles with a .45 caliber pistol. I would have thought there would be a lot of blood, but there was surprisingly little and what little there was, was directly under Charles' body and a small spot of blood on his left hand. Paramedics later said that if Alex had performed CPR on Charles like he claimed, that would have caused a lot of blood to exit Charles' body through the two bullet wounds. But, even knowing that Alex did not perform CPR, there should have been a lot of blood on the floor at least. There was not.

Charles had been wearing a cap and that cap ended up several feet behind him, against the wall behind where Charles had been standing when he was shot. How did it get from the top of Charles' head to where it was? I know there is some explanation for that. I just never heard what it was or even any idea of what it could have been. Did it come off during the altercation between Charles and Alex? Did the force of Alex's shot cause it to blow backwards? I don't think the latter is likely since Charles fell forward.

Charles had bruises and abrasions on his knees. It was explained that he received the bruises when he fell to the floor after Alex's first shot. I could understand that there could possibly be some small bruises caused by Charles falling to the floor, but the pictures shown in court showed substantial bruising and what appeared to me to be more like scrapes. Also, first responders found Charles lying flat on his back. If he fell forward onto his knees, I can't see how he ended up flat on his back. Where did those bruises come from? What is their significance? If Charles fell forward after being shot in the chest with a .45 why wasn't there blood on the floor in front of him?

The only blood I could see in the pictures of Charles's body was on his left hand. Since Charles was left-handed, that seems to make sense. He would have raised his hand to the wound he suffered right before he died.

Detectives said they found blood on the faucet in the kitchen, but they never said they tested it to see whose blood it was. Was it Alex's or Charles'? If there was blood on the faucet, why wasn't there blood anywhere else?

Alex claimed to have performed CPR at the direction of the 911 operator while he was waiting for medics. Chandler Fire Capt. Kent Keller previously testified that it didn't appear that Alex performed CPR. While on the phone with 911 the operator coached him and he claimed on the phone that he was performing CPR. Alex took 47 minutes from the time he shot Charles until he called 911. That's pretty damning. If he shot Charles in self-defense, he would have called immediately. He was waiting to make sure Charles was dead before he called. He needed Charles to bleed out.

The jury was shown pictures of a bag belonging to Alex, laying on the floor of the bedroom Alex had slept in the night before. The bag held the pistol, some surgical gloves and wet wipes. Did the police check the garbage cans or surrounding area for bloody gloves or wipes? They didn't say so in court. I thought that would have been important in their investigation. Why would Alex have a bag with gloves and wet wipes if he wasn't planning to shoot Charles? I would have thought that a bag with just a pistol, wet wipes and gloves would come off as suspicious to the investigating officers.

Alex had been a convicted felon. Convicted felons cannot be in possession of a firearm. Alex had some kind of deal where when he had completed his sentence and probation, the felony would be wiped from his record, so apparently it was legal for Alex to own a firearm. Was the gun registered to Alex? Where did he get it? Was he illegally in possession of it? Those questions never came up in court. Even though Alex had completed his sentence and probation, I had to wonder why. The only answer I can come up with is that it would show that the police were not at all thorough in their investigation. They had to have known Alex had been a convicted felon. Surely, they checked his background at least. Did it not occur to them that Alex might be illegally in possession of the gun?

Maybe I need to give the police the benefit of the doubt on this one point. Maybe Alex legally owned the gun and it didn't come up in court because it wasn't an issue. Alex owned the gun legally. Still, I would think the fact that he had at one time been convicted of a felony would have raised questions. Maybe it did.

There was a pair of what appeared to be slip-on shoes sitting neatly by the front door. Whose were they? Were they Tylees? They looked like they could be and that might explain why Tylee needed the flip flops LVD bought for her after they left the house. But, why did she leave them? Did she leave in a hurry not stopping to put on her shoes, or were the shoes bloody? I would have no reason to expect that they were bloody except that the whole scene appeared to be cleaned to me. I mean, it seemed like it was obviously cleaned. We find out in later testimony that the bat was clean with no fingerprints, there was no blood splatter, there was blood found on the kitchen faucet and the whole scene was just too neat. If there had been a fight, it would have been chaotic. Things would have been scattered.

We listened for what seemed like hours to a fingerprint expert. After waiting expectantly, at the end of her testimony, she said she was unable to extract fingerprints from the bat that Alex claimed Charles attacked him with. That was telling to me. The end of an aluminum bat is pretty smooth. If Charles had grabbed the end of the bat when Tylee was poking him with it, his fingerprints should have been all over it. Why weren't they? Had the bat been cleaned? Is it possible that Charles never held the bat?

So, a lot of unanswered questions. I had been hoping to get more of my questions answered in court. Like so much in this case, the more I listen and watch, the more questions I am left with.

I wrote in *Money, Power and Sex* that Lori, Tylee and JJ left the house to take JJ to school immediately after Charles was shot. They stopped after dropping JJ off to buy flip flops for Tylee. In the Arizona trial we were shown video of LVD at Walgreens paying cash for two pairs of flip flops. There were two sections of video. One of LVD walking through the front door into the store and another of her at the register paying. I can't tell in the video of her walking in if she has shoes on, but at the register I believe I see her drop one of the pairs to the floor and put them on. Was she barefoot? Why? And why doesn't she say she needed flip flops for herself? Did she and Tylee leave the house in a panic without their shoes, or was there blood on their shoes and she and Lori disposed of them along the way? Or did Alex clean them?

I'm still not sure if prosecutor Kay left a lot of evidence out or if the police in Arizona did a poor job investigating after Alex shot Charles. I am inclined usually to give the police the benefit of the doubt. The thing that sways me to the idea that they did a shoddy job investigating is that they let Alex go. They initially believed his story of self-defense in spite of evidence that appears to me to point more to murder.

The scene seemed extremely staged to me. It was too neat and clean and too many things just didn't add up. I believe that Alex spent the 47 minutes between the time he shot Charles and called 911, cleaning up and staging the murder scene. He probably even banged his head into a wall or something to cause the small cut on his head.

The scene was staged. There is no other conclusion that makes sense. What doesn't make sense to me is why it wasn't obvious to the investigators the day Charles was murdered.

Chad, Alex and LVD were like the Three Stooges committing murder. They were not smart and they were extremely naive. So, how did they outsmart the police in Chandler, AZ?

One could answer that they didn't. Chandler P.D. ended up arresting, prosecuting and convicting LVD. My answer to that is they did arrest and convict LVD, but only after Idaho charged and convicted her and only after three other innocent people were murdered.

Day Five 4-9-25,
Charles Had a Date

In her cross-examination of Det. Coons, LVD got him to say he didn't know when he wrote his report on the shooting of Charles. To me she was making inroads if her goal was to show the jury that the police might not have been as professional as we would have hoped. I could not, however, see how that helped her case.

She immediately lost the jury again anyway when she went on and on about the idea that Charles had been wearing a bamboo workout shirt. I believe her point was that it was a tight-fitting shirt and that would explain why there was no blood splatter. She was leaving out the fact that there was a divot caused by a bullet in the floor directly under Charles' body, proving Alex's second shot happened after Charles was flat on his back on the floor.

Every time LVD started making some points that could possibly sway the jury to her side, she blew it by making a ridiculous argument. I think the jury was starting to believe the Chandler police were incompetent simply because they *were* incompetent. Not because of anything LVD said. Then she tried to convince the jury that Charles' bamboo shirt stopped the bullet. Bamboo is such a strong fabric that it stopped the bullet from exiting through Charles' back. It wasn't the floor that stopped the bullet. The problem with that argument is that the bullet was laying on the floor under Charles' body and there was an obviously fresh divot in the floor. Not only was there clear testimony to that fact, there were pictures that clearly showed the bullet and the divot.

She unfairly kept calling Charles her husband. I'm sure she did that thinking the jury didn't know that she was married to Chad Daybell and Charles was no longer her husband.

Another difference I noticed at this point in the trial is that in Idaho the attorneys stayed behind their desks. If something needed to be handed to the judge or a witness a bailiff would do it. In Arizona the attorneys or their assistant would walk right up to the judge or witness and hand off whatever it was they were handing off.

It never came up if they swabbed LVD for gunshot residue. I was hoping to find out. It is possible that LVD shot Charles and Alex covered for her. Maybe she took the second shot. It might have at least crossed their minds. I think a good defense attorney might have brought it up just to show either that the investigation was not thorough, or that the police at the time of the shooting were not suspicious of LVD.

Nancy Jo Hancock who I got to meet and have a conversation with later was the next witness for the prosecution. Nancy Jo was an awesome witness and gained some fans.

She didn't have a lot of evidence to contribute that would help convict LVD, but I think she did have an effect on the jury and how they felt about Charles. She and Charles had met online and had been texting back and forth a lot leading up to their first date the night before Charles was murdered. She said Charles had been actively dating online and I could see that bothered LVD. Not surprising. She was having an affair with Chad Daybell, but how dare Charles go on a date.

Hancock's first and only date with Charles happened on July 10, the night before the morning Charles was murdered. She said her and Charles really hit it off and stayed up late talking. Charles was ecstatic to be seeing JJ and was looking for a house closer so he could see him more often. Charles talked kindly about LVD and her beliefs.

Hancock texted Charles the following morning to find out how his date with JJ went. When she got no reply, she called and he didn't answer. She was disappointed and it seemed odd to her since she thought the date went so well. As time went by, she convinced herself that it was just how it goes in the dating world, even though she knew Charles was too much of a gentleman to just blow her off and not answer and explain.

It wasn't until 6 months later that she finally found out that he had died. She immediately called the police to tell them about her date. When I heard that I knew for sure that the police didn't bother to investigate Charles' death at all. Her and Charles had been texting for a while leading up to their date and surely the police would have contacted the last person Charles was known to have been with.

LVD was vicious in her cross-examination. She said to Hancock:

"He was not in the process of divorce. Do you go on dates with married men?"

Hancock was just as good at standing up to LVD. She was witty and unphased. When LVD asked:

"What did *my husband* tell you about me?"

Judge Beresky immediately called for a break for lunch. This was one of the times where I understood why Judge Beresky wanted to give LVD's assistants the opportunity to tell her not to ask that question, but I wished he had just let things flow in the direction they were going. I would love to have heard Hancock's answer because I'm sure it would have been all about LVD's belief that she was a translated being who walked with Jesus and had lived many lives.

What would LVD's response have been? What would the jurors have thought? What would be the looks on their faces? It would have been priceless.

LVD did make things a little interesting after lunch though. She asked Hancock if she knew her brother, Adam Cox. Hancock got visibly flustered, I guess not expecting to be asked that question. She answered sheepishly that she had forgotten that she had had a date with Adam and that Adam had used a different name on the dating app. LVD then asked her:

"Do you know what perjury is?"

I didn't think Hancock perjured herself. She answered honestly when asked if she knew Adam, but she came close. She obviously didn't want to expose the fact that she had had a date with Adam, I'm guessing to protect Adam. Small world.

Again, a good attorney could have made more of this and possibly discredited the witness in the eyes of the jury. Adam lived in Texas. Charles lived in Arizona. Hancock lived in Arizona. How is it that Hancock had dated Adam when he lived in Texas and she lived in Arizona and then she coincidentally dated Adam's brother-in-law? There has to be more to that story. Hancock and Adam Cox were key witnesses for the prosecution and their credibility could have been brought into question.

Christina Atwood, a prior friend of LVD, was a pretty good witness for the prosecution. Atwood was Mormon and met LVD at church in 2010. She had visited LVD in Hawaii in 2019 and she knew Charles, JJ, Tylee and Colby. LVD told Atwood that Charles had been possessed by a dark spirit.

Atwood said she had known LVD before she had the zealotrous religious beliefs and had really looked up to her then. But things had changed. LVD had tried to get her to do "castings" and participate in weird rituals.

Atwood said she was put off by Alex. Something wasn't right with him. She heard him say more than once that he wished he could just kill Charles.

LVD told Atwood that she had crushed up JJ's meds and put them in Charles' energy drink mix. She quit spending time with LVD finally writing her off and not including her in her life. She said it was always all about Lori anyway and she was tired of it.

It was pretty damning testimony I thought and LVD didn't bother cross-examining her. I'm sure LVD knew it would not go well if she did.

One thing Atwood said brought a question to my mind: Tylee had a history of stomach issues. I've had a suspicion that LVD was somehow the cause of that. Was it from stress caused by Tylee's relationship with her mother or could LVD have been poisoning her? I would not put it past LVD to poison her own daughter. She would have done it to cause dependency. I explain LVD and Tylee's relationship in my previous two books, so I won't rehash it here, but I think the idea that LVD put Xanax in Charles' drink mix supports my idea.

It also makes me wonder about LVD's sister Stacey, Melani's mother. Could her health problems have been caused by someone poisoning her? They were strange, unexplainable and varied. It would seem far-fetched in any other context, but in the context of this case it makes perfect sense to wonder.

Day Six 4-10-25,
LVD Almost Exposed Herself to the Jury

I noticed the jury was dressing nicer than they had been. Are they realizing they are part of something worthy of more than shorts and a T-shirt or were they admonished to spruce it up a little bit?

LVD's brother, Adam Cox is on the stand. He is a professional pickle ball coach. He used to be a radio disc jockey. I know Adam and he is a nice guy above anything else. I do think he is in a little bit of denial about the family he grew up in, but who can blame him?

He did admit that LVD and Alex had a normal relationship growing up, but that they became oddly close.

My question for Adam is: are you just admitting to things in court or in public about your family that have already been exposed and hiding other things that aren't known? Or, do you sincerely believe your family was normal until LVD went down the religious rabbit hole? I wish he would open up, but I can't blame him for either being in denial or wanting to protect what is left of his family, so I don't push him too hard for an answer. While it doesn't matter in terms of his sister, it certainly does matter if we're to get to the bottom of *how* she could do what she did.

Either way, Adam is an important witness. A looking glass into LVD or as close as we can get to one. Adam's son had temporarily lived with Charles and LVD prior to 2019 so he must have trusted her then.

Adam liked Charles and said they had a normal brother-in-law relationship. They didn't hang out a lot, mainly at family functions.

Adam said that his brother, Alex had been excommunicated from the Mormon Church twice as an adult. LVD never worked. Around 2018 she started to try to convince him that she was translating into a celestial state and that she had more priesthood authority than men because of it.

Adam wasn't buying any of it and when LVD realized there was no way she was going to convince him, she just quit talking to him. When he tried to talk to other family members about LVD, they cut him out. They surely were in denial.

Charles told Adam about LVD's affair with Chad. Adam said that Charles was desperate to get her help. Charles was hoping for a family intervention, but Adam was the only one willing to support him. Adam even flew from his home in Texas to meet with Charles to try to help. Unfortunately, the meeting was set for the afternoon after Charles was murdered by LVD and Alex. When Adam landed, he texted Charles expecting

Charles to pick him up, but it was not to be, so Adam spent the night with his parents at their home.

At 7:35 am Adam got a text from Charles: "Al is here-at Lori's."

Adam texted back: "They are planning something."

Charles: "Absolutely."

Adam was upset at Alex and texted him, but got no response. He also was no longer getting a response from Charles. The last text that Adam sent to Charles was read by someone at 12:00 noon. It obviously couldn't have been read by Charles, so who read it and why wouldn't they have notified Adam that Charles had been shot by Alex? If it really had been self-defense, there would have been no reason not to tell Adam. In fact, knowing as much as I do about Alex and LVD, I would say they would have jumped at the opportunity to tell how Charles got so violent that Alex had to shoot him.

Adam was concerned about why Charles would not have followed through with their meeting. Especially since Charles paid for Adam's airfare, so obviously felt meeting with Adam was important. No one in the family bothered to tell Adam that Alex had shot Charles. He didn't find out until he expressed his concerns to a friend and the friend googled it and found out Charles had been shot to death.

Adam immediately called his mom and later went to her house to ask her:

"What's going on?"

He said that that meeting didn't go well.

In her cross-examination of Adam, LVD asked him when the last time they talked was and Adam answered that it was in 2018. She then asked:

"Did you personally see, hear or witness me conspire to murder my husband, Charles?"

Adam replied: "No."

I thought this was another opportunity for LVD to make some ground with the jury. Why didn't Adam put more effort into contacting Charles that morning? Didn't he think something went wrong when Charles showed up at LVD's house? He had the text from Charles telling him that Alex was there. Instead, she wasted her time asking Adam repeatedly if he remembered her green chili chicken enchiladas.

In her re-direct of Adam, Treena Kay asked him if he thought it seemed extreme that Alex would bring a gun to the house where JJ lived and Adam replied:

"No doubt in my mind that they killed him."

Even though she was given the opportunity, LVD did not re-cross. If Adam had no doubt that they killed him, why didn't he follow up with Charles that morning? LVD could have asked him that question.

The next witness called by the prosecution was Sarena Sharp. Sharp gave some insight into Chad and LVD's inner circle and their extreme religious beliefs. She had been a member of PaP in Arizona (Preparing a People). A prepper group focused on getting people prepared for the second coming of Christ.

She claimed she wasn't close enough to LVD to know about her and Chad's affair, but she did know a lot of people who LVD and Chad were associated with. She knew Chad, Melanie Gibb, Zulema Pastenes and Jason Mow. Mow did the "Warrior up" podcast with Melanie Gibb and LVD which was produced by Preparing a People in 2019. If you google him or any of the people who had been associated with Chad or LVD you won't find much. They have gone to great lengths to erase their history.

In a five-woman meeting of the inner circle Sharp said she heard LVD say:

"I don't believe we need to repent anymore."

Sharp said LVD went on to say she was changing physically and spiritually and went on to talk about "Castings." Castings were like ceremonies to cast out a demon in Jesus Christ's name, who had inhabited someone's body. She also told Sharp that Charles had been possessed by an evil zombie named Ned.

These things stood out to Sharp. She thought it was very unusual.

I was glad that at this point the jury was getting a taste of where LVD's mind was. They hadn't had much exposure to that, but I thought it was important to know.

LVD did her best to discredit Sharp in her cross-examination. She asked:

"Did you take an oath? Accountable to God?"

To which Sharp replied: "Yes."

LVD went on about having only 4 meetings in person and only 3 one on one conversations. Sharp said yes, but we had at least 10 phone conversations. I really couldn't see how any of this was helping LVD. Sharp never claimed they were close friends.

LVD went on to take issue with the idea that she said the word "Zombie." She really doesn't like that word for some reason. Sharp immediately replied that, yes LVD used that word at a girl's weekend in 2019. She sounded pretty sure of it and I was glad that someone called LVD on it. LVD asked if it could have been someone else who used the word. (She has used the word "zombie" multiple times and denied it in an interview she did with her son, Colby on his podcast.)

Things started to get interesting when LVD asked:

"Do you know of John the Revelator being translated? Was Elijah translated? The three Nephi's? It's not uncommon in Christianity to believe people can be translated."

Unfortunately, she stopped short of claiming she herself was a translated being, but the jury had to be catching on by this point.

Digital forensics expert William McDonald was next on the stand. After hearing a few different witnesses in three trials explain "Cellbrite" technology, I am actually starting to understand it. Well, sort of anyway. I get that police use Cellbrite to organize the information they gather on a device. I think it works kind of like AI. (Not that I understand AI all that well). There is too much information on a device that doesn't pertain to what the police are looking for. Chad and LVD used several different devices. It would take a lot of people years to sort through it all and glean the information the police are looking for and put it in an order that makes sense. Cellbrite is a program that somehow gleans the pertinent information and puts it in order and it does it quickly enough for the police to be able to use the information as evidence in a trial.

Okay, enough of that. The next witness was even less exciting. She was a fingerprint expert. She spent what seemed like forever describing her credentials. Isn't "fingerprint expert" enough? Anyway, after droning on and on about latent prints and friction ridge detail, she ended by saying she was unable to remove any prints from the bat. Really! I really don't know what her testimony was even about.

I do think that probably in any trial there are undertones or hints of a deeper meaning if anyone is interested. Not that anything this witness had to offer made any difference in the minds of the jurors, but I got something out of it. The bat had been cleaned. The witness explained that it was an aluminum bat with a smooth surface. If Charles had grabbed the end of the bat when Tylee was supposedly poking him with it, his prints would have been all over it. If you pick up any bat in any kid's bedroom, I bet it is covered with prints. She didn't say anything about it being cleaned, but the only conclusion is that it had been cleaned by Alex.

Prosecutor Kay made no mention of that. She could have asked in her cross-examination why there wouldn't be prints. My conclusion is she didn't ask because it would show a lack of effort on the part of the Chandler police, and that would weaken her case. I will go even further and say that Kay left out key witnesses and evidence that might have shown that Chandler Police were inept.

Kay Woodcock was next up for the prosecution. Woodcock is to me the most important witness to take the stand in this trial. She is Charles' sister and JJ's biological grandmother so she has lost more than anyone. She is also the one who would not relent when JJ and Tylee were missing. It was her idea to have Charles and LVD adopt and take over the care of JJ. She is angry at LVD and who can blame her? In spite of her anger that I know consumes her, she was able to maintain control of herself sitting in the witness stand in front of LVD.

There have been several people who we could call heroes in this case. We take the love of a grandmother for granted. Any grandmother who takes full time care of their grandchild is heroic, but most would do it if they had to. Kay Woodcock had to, but she did it with love and only the best interest of JJ in her heart. Giving JJ over to LVD and then having LVD murder him in the brutal way that she did hurt Woodcock in a way that the rest of us thankfully can't comprehend.

Watching Kay and Larry Woodcock in two Idaho trials and Kay Woodcock in two Arizona trials is one of the most heart wrenching experiences of my life. The anguish and unbridled sorrow mixed with anger I have seen on their faces is unmatched in my experience. Watching them from the jury box in Idaho brought tears to my eyes more than once.

Kay Woodcock explained that Charles was number three of six children in her family. Her sister Susan and brother Gerry were in the courtroom also. Charles and LVD adopted JJ in

2014 when JJ was two years old. Charles doted on JJ. Charles had sold annuities for twenty years and was very successful. He had received a college scholarship to play baseball and later was drafted into the minors by the Astros. He was a left-handed pitcher and left-handed batter. Unfortunately, a knee injury ended his career early.

Charles converted to Mormonism sometime after meeting LVD. Charles and LVD moved to Hawaii in 2014 and then to Phoenix in 2017. They had met in Texas. Woodcock was never as close to LVD as she was to Charles, but she had loved her. Charles and JJ visited Woodcock in 2018 and expressed concerns about LVD, but wouldn't say what they were. Later in 2019 Charles told Woodcock that he was concerned for his safety. LVD disappeared for 58 days in February and March of 2019 and left JJ with Charles. LVD didn't contact Charles or JJ at all during that time. Woodcock said LVD didn't want JJ anyhow. Woodcock offered to be JJ's nanny even though that meant she would have to leave her home in Louisiana and make huge sacrifices.

In early February of 2019 Charles switched the beneficiary of his life insurance policy from LVD to Kay Woodcock. June of the same year is the last time she saw Charles and May 18 is the last time she saw JJ. She was contacted by Chandler P.D. about the death of Charles. She told them that JJ was not safe with LVD. LVD had Charles' body cremated and FedExed his ashes to her. When the family went to Charles' apartment, they found that LVD cleaned out anything of value and left the family crap.

So, from Kay Woodcock's testimony we see that in the name of religion, LVD murdered Charles, took anything he owned that was of value, and abandoned her adopted son.

When LVD approached the witness stand to cross-examine Woodcock you could have heard a pin drop in the courtroom.

The idea that LVD, the woman who brutally murdered Woodcock's brother and grandson, had the audacity to address her, was offensive to me. I was sad that Woodcock had to go through that and angry that LVD would make her. It was the whole case in a nutshell. LVD couldn't care less who she hurt or how much she hurt them. It was all about her.

Fortunately, it didn't last long. LVD could see she was outmatched and I thought just maybe she was feeling just a little bit uncomfortable.

Day Seven 4-14-25,
Charles' Bamboo Shirt

As I did every morning, I counted the jurors as they entered the courtroom. We were one short. When the juror finally showed up, he said he forgot court started at 10:00. Is this person paying any attention at all? They were given a three-day weekend and court doesn't start until 10am. How much easier could Judge Beresky make it for them to do their duty?

Maricopa County Medical Examiner Dr. Deric Baumgartner was called to the stand to testify about the autopsy, cause of death and toxicology reports. His job would have been to establish a cause of death. It was multiple gunshot wounds. Baumgartner would not have been expected to determine if it was from self-defense or murder. Still, his testimony would provide evidence that would point to murder. We were shown detailed autopsy photos. They were both hard to look at and extremely interesting. A picture is worth a thousand words.

There were no abrasions or contusions on Charles' head. Charles' body was found lying on its back. If he had fallen backwards after being shot, there should have been some kind of bruising on the back of his head. There were abrasions on his chest and on his left hand. There was also blood on his left hand. There were abrasions on his knees. According to Dr. Baumgartner these abrasions were caused at the time of death or as he said perimortem.

There was stippling (gunpowder caused abrasions) on his chest indicating that the gun was from two to four feet from Charles when it went off. One of the bullets went directly through his heart. He could have lived only for seconds or possibly up to two minutes. During that time, he would have been able to speak, move and touch his wound with his hand.

Dr. Baumgartner explained that the abrasions on Charles' knees would have been consistent with Charles falling forward after having been shot. This idea was obviously questionable to me. Charles' body was found flat on its back. Not crumpled or facing forward like you would expect if he fell to his knees. Of course, he could have moved after falling, but two things made me think that's not what happened. First, the abrasions on Charles' knees looked to me more like scratches like you would expect if someone had been dragged. Second, if Charles fell forward and eventually ended up on his back, there would have been blood smeared on the floor. The small amount of blood that exited Charles' body was directly under the exit wound. The second shot was taken when Charles was flat on his back.

Nothing about the crime scene adds up. The only conclusion for me is that no one cared or paid enough attention to come to the correct conclusion that Alex and LVD murdered Charles in cold blood.

In her cross-examination LVD again made the ridiculous claim that Charles had been wearing an expensive bamboo shirt and that explained why the bullet didn't travel far after exiting his body. And again, she left out the part where the bullet was found under Charles' body and there was a divot in the floor where it struck.

In her re-direct Kay was able to get Baumgartner to say that a bamboo shirt wouldn't stop the bullet. The floor did.

This time when Judge Beresky asked if the jury had any questions for the witness, they did. A juror asked if there was blood in Charles' lungs and if he could have been alive when the second shot was taken. I have no idea what the significance of the first question was. I suppose that if Charles was dead when the second shot struck him, an argument could be made that it didn't count and Alex was within his rights to defend himself with lethal force. That's assuming of course, that we believe Alex shot Charles in self-defense in the first place. Or, I guess that the juror asking the question believes it.

Mark Sari investigated waste, fraud and abuse for the Social Security Administration. He investigated the payments LVD received after Charles died. On 8/12/19 she met with S.S. and told them that her and Charles were living together at the time of his death. She later neglected to tell them that she married Chad on 9/5/19 while she continued collecting Charles' death benefit.

In her cross-examination LVD tried to convince the jury that S.S. had made a mistake on her application. She asked Sari if he had seen her application and he said he had reviewed all of the documents. Nice try. LVD, the one who claims to be on a higher spiritual plane than the rest of us, has no problem lying and doing her best to twist the truth. I guess if you walk with Jesus and are pilloried for it, you have to do whatever it takes to defend yourself against the mere mortals attacking you.

In her re-direct Kay asked if there was any record of LVD notifying S.S. and Sari replied that there was zero notification and said:

"I did not miss it."

The trial is getting a little monotonous for me at this point. Most of these witnesses have one or more significant points to make, but it takes a long time to get to the point. I understand that there is protocol and witnesses can't just get on the stand and make statements. Foundation has to be established. So, on we go.

Banner Life Insurance Company employee Robin Smith-Scott processes death claims. She stated on the stand that all requests for payment phone calls are recorded. Prior to March, 2019 LVD was the beneficiary of Charles life insurance and after that date Kay Woodcock was.

On 7/15/19, four days after Charles was murdered, LVD placed a call to Banner Life Insurance. We listened to the call in court. We heard her say:

"Well, he was shot. It was an accident."

When asked who the beneficiary was, LVD replied: "Um, it's me."

Her first answer was an outright lie. I think she assumed she was the beneficiary when she made the call. She found out differently when she received a reply by email three days later stating that she was not the beneficiary.

At this point LVD seemed to be losing heart. She was getting nowhere trying to lie and manipulate witnesses. Treena Kay had done her job well and the witnesses were prepared for LVD's questions. They were not allowing her to hoodwink them.

Forensic scientist Jeff Moeber was asked by Kay if the bullets matched the gun and he replied that they did. That seemed pretty straight forward, but LVD had apparently received a second wind.

It's one thing to look the part of an attorney. It's another thing to actually do the job of an attorney. It was obvious by this point that LVD was doing her best to play a part. She was trying to look smart. It became apparent to me that this was all just a show to her. She knew she couldn't win, so she was just enjoying putting everyone through this trial just for her own entertainment.

I suppose it did beat rotting in a jail cell, but at what cost to everyone else? This whole thing is nothing more than a joke to her, which means we're all just a joke to her. Grandma Kay Woodcock is a joke to her, her victims are a joke to her and the taxpaying citizens are apparently a joke to her also.

Anyway, a lot of questions about how long it takes to do the tests on the bullets and pistol to determine if they are a match. Who requested the analysis. When was the test requested? She was just going step by step through her notes she wrote when Kay was asking the questions, repeating what Kay had just gone over with the witness.

She did ask about the location of the casings. Remember, I am suspicious about where they ended up. I was disappointed though when she let it drop. She missed another opportunity to do the one thing that might help her case; show incompetence or dishonesty on the part of the police.

I guess a juror was catching on to how the casings got to where they got though. I'm glad someone is paying attention.

When given the opportunity by Judge Beresky, the juror asked:

"If Alex had held the gun sideways, could the casings have gone to his left?"

That's a possibility I had not thought of. If a shooter held the pistol sideways parallel to the floor the casing would be ejected straight up. However, he would have to have held it at an exaggerated angle, more than parallel to the floor for the casings to be ejected to his left. Also, if the direction of the barrel changed when Charles fell to the floor and Alex took his second shot, the casings would still have taken very different paths even if the pistol were held sideways. The first shot taken while Charles was upright would have sent the casing straight up. The second shot taken while Charles was laying on the floor would have sent the casing forward.

When Chandler P.D. Officer Kasandra England took the stand, I recognized her immediately as the officer who interviewed Tylee at the police station right after Charles was shot. I've watched that video more times than I can count trying to gain insight into Tylee. A side effect of that is that I gained insight into the Chandler Police Department and the standards they hold their officers to.

I'm aware that some of the best officers we know of were renegades. At least that's true in the movies. Think of Dirty Harry and Joe Pistone. Officer England however, doesn't strike me as someone in the same league as those two. She strikes me as someone who is simply unaware that it might be less than impressive for a police officer to sport a "whale tale". If you don't know what I'm referring to, ask your teenage daughter or anyone who grew up in the 2000s.

Anyway, as the interview concludes and Officer England stands up, her thong underwear can clearly be seen rising above her pants in the back. If you doubt me, YouTube the interview. I could go on, but I'll just say in my old-fashioned mind it points to the overall standards, or I should say lack of standards held by the Chandler P.D.

England was on duty the day Charles was shot and she responded to the call. When she got to the house Alex was sitting on the curb talking to Officer Krauthiem. He didn't appear to her to be in any way agitated or upset. She noticed LVD and Tylee across the street, but did not yet know who they were. When she interviewed them later, they were nonchalant. (there's that word again). England was the one who drove the van and transported LVD to the police station for questioning. On the way she told LVD that Charles was dead and LVD replied that she knew that because she was there.

To me that sounds like she was saying she was in the house or how would she know he was dead? She told other officers she left before Alex shot Charles.

In spite of her conflicting stories and the fact that LVD showed no emotion at the house or on the way to the police station, LVD was taken to the Family Advocacy Center and treated more like a victim than a perpetrator or even a person with pertinent information that could help the police understand the truth of what happened.

England went on to testify that LVD told her Charles had sent her threatening texts, but LVD never showed them to her. England didn't think to ask to see them? LVD went on to tell England that she picked up Charles' phone. Charles screamed at her to give it back and chased her around. LVD claims that that was when Charles came after her with the bat.

Kay asked:

"Did you ever ask her why she didn't just give Charles back his phone?"

England replied:

"No, I did not."

In all of this LVD never called 911. Why? Wouldn't any normal person call 911? Even if we accept the idea that she left the house because she was scared of Charles, surely, she would call 911 when she left. It's all so transparent and obvious that Alex and LVD had a plan to murder Charles and claim self-defense. Unfortunately, the Chandler P. D. was gullible enough to believe their totally absurd story.

And that was it. When they were done "interviewing" LVD and Tylee, they drove them back to the house. LVD continued to be unaffected and chatty on the drive back. She gave no acknowledgement to what had just happened. Her brother just shot her husband in her house. Even if it were self-defense, surely a normal person would be upset. Why couldn't the police see that?

LVD's first question for England in her cross-examination showed that things might get a little more entertaining. She asked:

"'Nonchalant', what's your definition?" Not again!

Then:

"Do you have a degree in psychology?" What?

"Ty needs meds that were inside the house." So?

"But you were aware that she needed her panic attack medication?" Again, what's the point?

LVD said everyone was being calm. No one was running around being hysterical. LVD is testifying herself. Judge Beresky and Treena Kay are giving LVD rope. Is it so she can hang herself? I'm guessing so. She is contradicting herself in front of the jury. She is also getting confrontational with the witness.

England said she was certified to interview children. No mention in whatever class she took of how to dress appropriately in front of children, I guess.

(At this point in my writing I'm wondering if anyone is getting offended by my inability to hide my sarcastic criticism of Officer England. If so, you might think it old-fashioned of me to worry about how someone dresses. Maybe it is old-fashioned and maybe it's not. I think a standard of professionalism is important. If you think I am unfairly attacking a female officer, I am not. I would be just as critical of a male officer wearing pants that rode low on his hips exposing his underwear and I think it is just as ridiculous and unprofessional.)

LVD tried to bring up the idea that Tylee told her that her meds were in the house. It was an obvious objection by Kay because anything Tylee would have said would be hearsay. This is where I was hoping a juror would ask why Tylee wasn't testifying. I guess it would have been hard for them to think to ask that question. For all they knew, Tylee might testify later.

The Marshall sitting off to the side appeared to almost fall out of his chair. Did he fall asleep? Who could blame him?

Day Eight 4-15-25,
The State Rests its Case

A lot of family members of victims are in court today: Kay Woodcock, JJ's grandmother; Julie Brooks, Tammy Douglas Daybell's cousin; Gerry Vallow, Charles Vallow's brother; Brandon Boudreaux, LVD's niece's ex-husband; Megan Connor, LVD's cousin (not there to support LVD. Just like in Idaho, no one was there to support her). There were also a few victim's advocates.

We begin the day with Judge Beresky asking LVD if she has any outstanding subpoenas. He is asking because he can see that the prosecution is winding down their case. If LVD plans to call witnesses, she has to subpoena them and give them time to get to Phoenix. He has been trying to help her with this since before the trial started. I've watched Judge Beresky and LVD discuss it before. Beresky asks her directly if she has subpoenaed her witnesses. LVD goes around and around not directly answering the question. Beresky, although trying to help her, finally gives up and moves on.

LVD has been obstinately disorganized, I think on purpose. She claimed she would bring evidence that would show her innocence. I know LVD and I know or at least know about her potential witnesses. There is no one out there who can help her case and she knows it. Judge Beresky gave up and finished what was turning into an argument by telling LVD she was out of time.

Getting back to LVD's cross examination of England, LVD asked what the police did with Charles' phone after LVD gave it to England. England replied that she sent it off to Sgt. Allness in the Crimes Division. LVD began testifying again as she asked if threatening messages existed on the phone and did you know that Charles had a $2million life insurance policy on me? More propaganda to confuse the truth.

I'm getting a little worried. I don't think the jury trusts the State. I think they are seeing the holes even though Kay is doing her best to wind her way around them. The jury not trusting the State is the one thing that can help LVD. If they think the investigation was flawed and if they don't trust the police, it will surely work in LVD's favor and might even get her an acquittal.

When Judge Beresky asked if the jury had any questions, they did have one: Was Charles' rental car searched?

It's a good question, but I wish they would think to ask about the blood on the faucet, did they check LVD for gunshot residue? Did they look for bloody rags and gloves in the garbage? Why was there no blood splatter? How did the casings end up together to Alex's left? Why did Tylee need flip flops? Why did LVD and Tylee leave with Charles' phone? Why didn't LVD call the police? I could go on.

We get a clearer picture of the timeline from Chandler P.D. Detective Ariel Werther. She looked very nervous on the witness stand and my thought was that wouldn't help convince the jury to trust the State.

She used cell phone location and GPS to track LVD's movements on the morning Charles was murdered. (I don't say allegedly because this trial ends in a murder conviction for LVD.) She also found out that LVD was in possession of Charles' wallet and hotel room key. I guess we can't read too much into that. She and Charles were married even though they were estranged and LVD was having an affair. But, when did she take Charles' wallet? Was it after he was shot or before?

On 7/11/2019 at 8:36am Chandler P.D. received a 911 call from Alex saying he shot his brother-in-law. Five minutes later at 8:41am the police showed up at LVD's house. LVD showed up at 8:48am and was asked to stay across the street away from Alex. There were 12 minutes between the 911 call and

LVD showing up at the scene. At 7:54am LVD had been caught on video at the Burger King drive through.

The next day police got the key card from LVD for Charles' room at the Hampton Inn. They impounded his backpack, suitcase and laptop. Next, they checked with seven different Walgreens stores until they found the one LVD went to buy flip flops. They were able to retrieve the receipt and video of LVD coming into the store.

Nothing all that exciting in all of that. I think it just shows that LVD left the scene and didn't call 911.

Detective Nathan Duncan, the Case Detective took the witness stand and kind of summarized the case and filled in a few gaps. Alex did own the gun he used to shoot Charles.

I was thinking at the time that that would be a felony for Alex since he was a convicted felon. Federal law and most state laws prohibit convicted felons from owning a firearm. That was not addressed in court and what difference would it make anyway? As I stated earlier, after I did some research, I found that Alex's felony had been swiped after he served his sentence.

Charles' phone left LVD's house at 7:49am and the 911 call came in at 8:36am. Charles lay dying and bleeding on the living room floor for 47 minutes.

As soon as Det. Duncan was done testifying the State rested its case. LVD filed a motion for acquittal which was quickly denied. Standard procedure for defense attorneys.

Day Nine 4-17-25, Where's the Evidence?

LVD tells Judge Beresky she would not be presenting any evidence. No witnesses will testify for her. I guess she doesn't have any evidence after all which would show her innocence. She couldn't even find one person to testify on her behalf. I'm not surprised. It was all just a big show. A hollowed-out shell of a woman lying to everyone in spite of the obvious truth.

In the end it took the jury only three hours to convict LVD of Conspiracy to Commit Murder of Charles Vallow.

15

THE STATE OF ARIZONA VS LORI VALLOW DAYBELL
(CONSPIRACY TO COMMIT MURDER OF BRANDON BOUDREAUX)

'm not going to go through the whole trial of LVD and Alex's attempt to murder Brandon Boudreaux. I wasn't able to attend the trial and it was a lot of the same testimony that we have already heard.

I do not want to diminish the importance of justice for Brandon however. LVD and Alex ambushed him and tried to murder him in cold blood, giving him no chance to defend himself.

Brandon was a good family man. At the time of the attempt on his life, he was married to Melani Boudreaux and had four children. He had been doing his best to hold his family together while his wife, Melani was going down the same religious rabbit hole as her Aunt Lori.

The effects of the attempt on his life didn't end when Alex missed his shot. Brandon says he and his family basically went into hiding expecting another attempt. He didn't know if his children were safe either. He did know or at least believe that Melani, the mother of his children, was behind the attempt and she had 50% custody of them. Life was a combination of chaos and fear.

Imagine having your life squared away. You are married to a woman you love, you have a good career that you love, you love your church, you have four beautiful children, and your extended family is supportive and loving. You go to work in the morning and when you come home your wife is a good stay at home mom. You have worked hard your whole life for this.

But slowly something changes. Your wife isn't taking as much interest in the children. She is spending more time at church than with them. She starts to look at you differently. You become her adversary. Nothing you say gets through to her and according to her, it's all your fault. You fight for your marriage. It's all you ever dreamed of.

Before you know what is happening you are in the middle of a contentious divorce and fighting to stay in your children's lives. You become concerned for your safety and the safety of your children. The police are involved and your life has turned into a nightmare. Your wife is doing anything she can to hurt you and ruin you and you don't know why.

She tries to destroy your reputation. She tells members of your church that you are gay just to hurt your standing in the church and make people think you are something you are not. She tries to ruin your career. The lies she tells about you are unending.

This is what they did to Brandon. They destroyed his life and then tried to murder him. Nothing could be more cold hearted. Well, maybe brutally murdering your own children and burying them in your lover's backyard.

But this is Lori Vallow Daybell. She is a monster. She is one of the most dangerous criminals to ever walk this earth. This is why she has been convicted by three different juries. She is very capable of convincing people to murder for her. She does it for her own selfish purposes. And the scariest thing about her is she couldn't care less. Sympathy or empathy do not reside in her.

But the important question in this case is different. LVD conspired with her brother, Alex to murder Brandon. Okay, by the time of this trial that much is all but a given. No one doubts that she tried to have Brandon killed. No one doubts that she tried to ruin his life. No one doubts that she wanted everything that was his. No one doubts that LVD is a ruthless and cold-blooded murderer.

But, why? Why did she do all of those things? What was in it for her? What would her motive have been?

I can think of three things that would have motivated LVD to murder Brandon:

1) Money: Melani and Brandon were selling their home due to their impending divorce.
They were planning to split the proceeds 50/50. If Brandon died, Melani would get 100%. The attempt on Brandon's life happened right before the sale of the house was due to close. Could LVD have thought that Melani would share that money with her? I think it's a very good possibility.

2) To help Melani: Could LVD have just been doing a "good deed" to help out her Niece?
Was she trying to help Melani solve her marital problems by murdering Brandon? I think it's possible, but I think there would have had to be something in it for LVD. What would LVD have had to gain? A loyal follower. Someone beholden to her. Someone she would have complete control over. Someone she could blackmail if she needed to. Another "Alex" who would do whatever horrific act LVD required. It's actually a terrifying thought, but I think it has merit. What were LVD's plans? Were others going to die? Did she need more soldiers to complete her mission? I think so. I think in LVD's mind, she could control everything. She found a way to collect Social Security benefits from dead husbands. She could collect life insurance money. I think that in her simple mind, she thought she could get away with all of it. It never dawned on her that people would catch on to her. Her only problem was that money had a way of running out or never being enough. Especially in LVD's hands. She wasn't the best money manager. I think it goes even deeper than that though. I think LVD had a belief that she had a mission from God to gather souls. How many would God have required of her? She was just getting started.

3) Hatred of men: LVD hates men. She does. She thinks she is above men and that she can manipulate them to do her bidding. She has no respect. But why?
That's a big question. Was she abused by her father? We don't know. We do know she was raised in a very patriarchal family and a very patriarchal church. She had a history of manipulating and using men. She had

been married five times, so we know she had a hard time relating to men. Men were her pawns. A man was only in her favor if she could manipulate him to do what she wanted him to do. She despised any man she couldn't control and was okay with destroying any man she no longer had a use for. Her brother Alex is the best example of that. Possibly Chad also.
We think Chad was the one with the ideas and LVD was following along. Looking back over everything, I'm not so sure. It might have been the other way around. If I'm right, she destroyed Chad also. She used her feminine wiles and manipulative skills to get Chad to do what she wanted. That included finding reasons to kill her children who she was tired of, and burying them in his backyard. Chad and Alex were duped, manipulated and used as pawns by LVD.

The jury was even quicker this time. It took them 30 minutes to convict LVD of Conspiracy to Commit Murder of Brandon Boudreaux.

WAS IT CHAD OR WAS IT LORI?

Looking back on it all, one thing becomes obvious to me that I have to admit wasn't obvious until now. Now that I have been to three trials and written three books and basically immersed myself in trying to understand the mind of a serial murderer.

This might shock the conventional thinking about this case and it certainly goes against the psychologists I have listened to who have talked about it, but Chad was duped. His kids are right. At least about some of it. Lori Vallow Daybell was the ringleader, the manipulator, the catalyst who brought forth the murders of Charles, Tammy, Tylee and JJ and the attempted murder of Brandon.

Wait a minute. Before you throw my book down in disgust, hear me out. I watched the video of Chad's daughter Emma laughing while Det. Hermosillo and others were literally exhuming JJ's remains in her backyard. I watched her laugh with Chad that day and was disgusted by her. I've seen her and her brother Garth intentionally lie to protect their father multiple times. I'm not forgiving anyone. There is plenty of blame to go around. I'm just saying that I have come to realize that LVD was the driving force, the one with the plan. And she had it all planned before she ever met Chad.

Chad is a weird guy and dangerous enough that I'm glad he's on death row, but LVD put him there. He was fine with having Alex murder his wife, Tammy. He may have even held Tammy down on their bed while Alex suffocated her, but he never would have done it if not for LVD. She came into his life, seduced him and manipulated him. She put ideas into his head.

Sure, Chad originally had the ideas of castings, zombies, near death experiences and the light and dark scale. (none of it original to him, but he had those ideas before LVD came into his life) But, Chad was a simple guy. He was living in a Harry Potter world hoping to get lucky at a PaP conference when LVD showed up. He was never really going to follow through with any of it. Certainly not to the point of murder.

When Chad and LVD met at a PaP convention in 2018 and Chad told LVD they had been married in a previous life and she seemed to fall for it, it was actually LVD who was baiting Chad. She ran with it. She knew better. She searched him out and was there in front of him on purpose. She was prepared to win him over. She had studied him, read his books and knew what his beliefs were. She was also smart enough to know that this was a man who could be molded by her. She knew he wasn't smart and she knew he was willing to lie and cheat to elevate himself in the eyes of his followers.

One bit of testimony I heard in LVD's trial in Idaho sticks out to me now. Chad was married to Tammy while having an affair with LVD. LVD was getting impatient with Chad. She wanted Tammy out of the picture so she and Chad could be married. She said she was tired of waiting and told him she was moving on and he should go on with his life with Tammy. LVD had been waiting for Chad, pressuring him to take care of Tammy so she and Chad could begin their life together. I will bet that Lori set up the murder of Tammy, sending Alex over and telling Chad Alex was coming and he better go along. Remember, by this time JJ and Tylee were buried in Chad's backyard. LVD could easily have used that fact to coerce Chad.

On the witness stand in Chad's trial, his daughter Emma and son Garth told us it was all LVD's doing. She and her brother Alex buried Tylee and JJ in their backyard. At the time I could not understand why they would lie for the man who murdered their mother. I still don't understand, but I'm not sure that they were knowingly lying. Or at least, what they were saying may have been partly true.

LVD and her brother Alex were the true murderers, the ones who enjoyed murdering to get what they wanted. Chad just saw what to him was a smoking hot blond woman, who for some reason was interested in him. Sadly, he was just unable to see through that until it was too late. Alex actually committed the murder of Tylee and Chad was complicit. In his mind, he had no choice but to go along with everything that came after.

And, that explains why they buried Tylee and JJ in Chad's backyard. There were plenty of less likely spots to bury a body in that part of Idaho. Putting them in Chad's backyard kept Chad loyal to LVD. There would be no way that Chad could convince the police that he wasn't closely involved.

Too bad for Chad that he didn't have a more creative lawyer. Someone who could have presented a case that might have at least saved Chad from the death penalty. John Prior did try to claim that Chad was duped by LVD, but he didn't present a very compelling case.

If I'm right about LVD (and I think I am), what else was on her agenda? Who else would have been murdered if she hadn't been found out? And did she murder people before Chad came into her life?

There are many suspicious coincidences in her life. A lot of people died of questionable things. Starting with her baby sister (who died before LVD was born), then her older sister, then her husband Joseph Ryan, then her brother Alex and then nosy neighbor Eldon Clawson. Are there others? I bet there are.

I think LVD left a path of destruction as she moved through her life. She is a cold blooded maniacal serial murderer with no remorse or compassion. She used brother Alex as her hitman and then probably murdered him too. Alex actually enjoyed murdering people. In that sense Chad is another of her victims.

What if Chad and LVD had never met? What would Chad's life look like? Would he have committed murder? He most likely wouldn't be sitting on death row. Would Tammy still be alive? Would his family be intact? There is no way to know the answer to these questions, but I wonder, as Chad sits hour after hour, day after day, waiting for his sentence to be carried out, if he wishes he had never met LVD. Was it worth it? I'm sure he had some exciting times with her, but I hope at least that he is feeling some remorse and regret.

LVD is never going to feel those things. Chad will eventually be put to death by the state of Idaho. Given enough time, I think Chad will eventually come to terms with the reality of what he and LVD did. I think I could see it in his demeanor in court in his trial in Idaho. He knows his soul is lost. He will never be forgiven for what they did. LVD's soul was lost a long time ago. We may never know what snapped in her mind or what caused it, but she is truly beyond redemption.

I do think Chad tried to convince Tammy that they should live a life of polygamy. He would have told her it was for a higher purpose, but he wouldn't have done it for his standing with Christ or because he believed it would put him on a higher spiritual plane. He would have done it to have more sex with more women.

From what I have learned about Tammy, I think she would have been offended by the idea, and I also think it would have caused a rift in their marriage. I also think it's probably why Chad predicted her early demise. Not that he had plans to murder her, but that in his simple mind, he either just hoped she would die young so he could go on with his pursuit of other women, or maybe even that he thought that he had some kind of spiritual power or influence over who lived or died.

SENTENCING

n 2023 Lori Vallow Daybell's sentencing in Rexburg, Idaho happened at a very inconvenient time for me. The same goes for the sentencing in Arizona, but I would not miss it. We scheduled a flight from Boise to Phoenix the night before the sentencing and we would fly home the afternoon of the sentencing.

I was concerned that we would miss out on some opportunities to talk to people whom I wanted to talk to. I did, but I did not leave Arizona disappointed. In fact, I left there uplifted.

When we arrived in Phoenix the evening before the sentencing my wife and I decided to walk by the courthouse. A line was already forming and one of the occupants of the line was someone I got to know during the Chad Daybell trial. She seemed nervous that I wasn't in that line and I have to say she was making me nervous that I wasn't in that line.

As it turned out, I probably should have been in that line. I'm perfectly capable of sleeping just about anywhere and I could have slept in a chair in front of the Maricopa County Courthouse.

I thought I had an *in* though. I had been told by a family member that they had reserved a seat for me. I know very well that that family member did his best to reserve me a seat and thought he had reserved me a seat, but in the end, it didn't work out. I think there were just too many people way more important than me that deserved to be in the courtroom more than me. I hope he knows I understand that. It was a day he had been waiting for for six years. It was his day, not mine.

Looking back on it I have to admit to myself that even though I never asked him to reserve me a spot, I was selfish for even allowing him to tell me he would do it. I should have refused his offer and stood in line.

The next morning, thinking I had a seat reserved, I made the mistake of still not getting in the line. I could have, I just didn't think I needed to. When the family went into the courtroom and I wasn't included, I thought I would not get in. I finally got in line, thinking I had no chance. As it turned out, my wife and I were the last ones let in. Whew! After all I had been through, not getting in would have been a disaster.

Long before the trial started, I contacted Judge Beresky's clerk. I made the argument that I was media and I wanted a pass so I wouldn't have to wait in line or worry whether or not I would get in. Of course, I didn't get a pass. I didn't expect to, but it was worth a try. If you look up "media" in the dictionary it includes writing books. By definition I am media, but the court doesn't see it that way regardless of the opinion of the dictionary.

I got a chuckle out of it one day though. I happened to be talking to someone who had a media credential and free access to the courtroom. He was a reporter who you would know. One of those guys whose face is everywhere it seems, but nothing all that meaningful comes out of it. Just sound bites and headlines. Anyway, I mentioned to him that according to the dictionary I am a member of the media. His scoff was so unchecked as he bridled and with disdain in his voice said: "You're not media." I was so glad I brought it up. It was priceless.

It was hard watching family members give their victim's impact statements, but it was also good to see them finally get to tell LVD what they think of her. I know that as heart wrenching as it was, it was good for them. I won't go through and repeat here what they said. Even though it's public and you can look it up and watch it, it seems personal to me. Like it's not my place to share what they said or how they said it.

I will just say that I have gotten very close to some of them and I have seen their anguish many times. Their loss is unrepairable. For most of us, it's unimaginable.

Of course, LVD was given the opportunity to address the judge just as she did in Idaho. I won't repeat any of what she said either, for totally different reasons. It was all B.S. anyway. The best part of her allocution statement was when Judge Beresky interjected when she said something that was untrue. He was obviously out of patience with her. Judges are supposed to be as impartial as possible, but they are human and he could see firsthand the suffering she caused. I think some human emotion overcame his desire to remain impartial and I think his little corrections of her felt good to everyone in his courtroom.

In Treena Kay's rebuttal she very thoroughly went point by point through what LVD had said stating that a tragedy would have been an accident. Not premeditated, not intentional and not conspiring.

Kay went on to say LVD was a "cold blooded murderer. She twisted religion and fashioned it." She used religion to gain "money and sex."

Kay mentioned Melani again saying it was all about money to her also. She talked about the emotional harm LVD caused Charles' family and Brandon's family.

"She sentenced these families to emotional harm."

In the end LVD was sentenced to two consecutive life sentences in Arizona. She would serve out her time in Idaho though. If for some reason Idaho released her, she would begin her sentences in Arizona.

The family invited my wife and I to a gathering they were having after the sentencing. There I finally got to meet Todd Trahan (JJ's biological father), Brandon Boudreaux and Prosecutor Treena Kay. I also got the opportunity to visit with a lot of people I had become associated with in writing my books. It was an uplifting time, but our flight was due and we had to cut it short.

I had thought that going to the sentencing would provide me with a sense of closure. Rushing to the airport and getting on the plane back home to Boise, I felt anything but closure. As it turns out, it's the thing I least expected when I was first called in for jury duty. The deeper I dive into this case and the more I learn, the more I realize that religious zealots have roots in our culture and that they are evil. They murder, they enslave, they rape, they torture and they do it all in the name of God. The truth is they are the worst kind of criminals. They prey on those who are weaker than them. And they do it to fulfil their own disgusting desires.

It is admittedly unusual for a woman to do the horrendous things LVD did and that's the biggest reason we're so interested in her. Men commit the majority of murders in our country. In the U.S. only 8.6% of serial killers are women. Women kill mainly for money. Most of the women and children who are murdered are murdered by those who we expect to protect them.

This is my last book about Chad Daybell and Lori Vallow Daybell. I have no intention of doing any more research into them or their crimes. Even if Melani Boudreaux or any other of Chad and LVD's inner circle are charged for their crimes, I will stay out of it.

My hope is that my writing has caused us to question the world we live in. Maybe look at things in a different way. I hope I have influenced people to finally do something about the FLDS and other religious fundamentalist groups who aren't what they claim to be. Even though I don't plan to write any more about it, if I get any opportunity to expose them, I will do it. Others who are smarter and more experienced than me have tried though and on it goes.

Thinking back on it all I guess Idaho prosecutors Rob Wood and Lindsey Blake had it right all along. It all really does come down to money, power and sex.

ACKNOWLEDGEMENTS

This third book was in most ways a solo endeavor. I didn't pester family members of the victims for information because this book is more about the history that led us to where we are in the present.

I didn't question the usual suspects in the media as much as I did for the first two books.

I didn't have as much access to the prosecution, law enforcement and the judge as I did in Idaho.

No factual book can be written, however, without a lot of information from many different sources. Even though I don't directly quote many of those sources, I have gained accumulated knowledge over the course of my adult life and I want to acknowledge some of that here.

Also, if you are interested in the subject matter of this book, I recommend you read the books I list below:

Under the Banner of Heaven
John Krakauer

Story Hustler: Murder, Mayhem, PTSD
Mike Watkiss

Prophet's Prey
Sam Brower

Breaking Free, How I Escaped Polygamy, the FLDS Cult, and My Father, Warren Jeffs
Rachel Jeffs

Silenced in the Name of God
Stephanie Taylor

Massacre at Mountain Meadows
Ronald W. Walker, Richard E. Turley Jr., Glen M. Leonard

Orrin Porter Rockwell: Man of God, Son of Thunder
Harold Schindler

Kingdom of Nauvoo
Benjamin E. Park

Vengeance is Mine
Richard E. Turley, Barbara Jones Brown

The Mountain Meadows Massacre
Juanita Brooks

Blood of the Prophets
Will Bagley

I would also like to thank:

Megan Connor and her YouTube Channel- Third_Verse. Megan shared her vast knowledge with me, helped edit the book and has always been a positive voice and a good friend.

Tricia Griffith and her Websleuths Radio Podcast. Tricia has promoted my books, shared information and put up with me on her podcast more times than I can count.

My wife, known to a lot of you as Tom's Wife Susan. She has not only helped me with editing, promoting and just all around supporting what I'm doing like she always has, but she also puts up with my frustrations and rants.

Many other people have promoted my books, had me on their podcasts, shared information or just given me encouragement. I am thankful to all of them.

ABOUT THE AUTHOR

This is Tom's third book about the brutal, uncalled for murders of Tylee Ryan, JJ Vallow, Charles Vallow and Tammy Daybell. When Tom's jury service in the Lori Vallow Daybell trial in Idaho in 2023 was over, he knew there was a lot more to this story. Tom had a burning question in his mind that would not let him rest: Not why, but *how* could a wife and  mother brutally murder her spouse, her children and the wife of her lover?

He knew it was a complex question and there was no easy answer. Whatever the answer was, Tom was committed to finding it. After two years of research, writing and contemplation Tom has finally answered the question. You may not like the answer, but Tom believes that our culture created Lori Vallow Daybell.

Tom says that life is full of twists and turns. You have to go where it takes you and you never know where that will be. He plans to continue writing, but no more true crime. He is currently working on a children's book. He says it's therapy for him. A complete work of fiction that will be light hearted and fun. No more tears, no more research and no more sitting in a courtroom.

Tom is not sorry that he was called into jury service for the trial in Idaho. He is thankful for the experience of watching the justice system in two totally different states in action. He is immensely proud of the police, prosecution and court system in Idaho. He is thankful for people in the media who have supported his writing. He is thankful for the family members of the victims who trusted him enough to open up and share their lives with him. He is extremely thankful for the friends he made and plans to continue to build those relationships.

www.ingramcontent.com/pod-product-compliance
Lightning Source LLC
Chambersburg PA
CBHW021525150726

47990CB00006B/2092